编写委员会

总 主 编：郁云峰

副总主编：于天琪　陈维昌

主　　编：郭伟刚　潘国庆　刘博

副 主 编：付世州　翁海明　王玉云

编　 者：王正伟　陶宝春　王琳　崔富义　牟彦春　韩霁

编辑委员会

主　　　任：陈维昌

副 主 任：付彦白

项目负责人：付彦白

项 目 秘 书：武传霞

项 目 审 定：王俊毅

项 目 编 辑：武传霞　王巧燕　方兴龙　赫栗　张彪

专家委员会（按音序排列）

陈曼倩	哈尔滨职业技术大学	崔永华	北京语言大学
梁赤民	中国-赞比亚职业技术学院	梁　宇	北京语言大学
刘建国	哈尔滨职业技术大学	宋继华	北京师范大学
宋　凯	有色金属工业人才中心	苏英霞	北京语言大学
赵丽霞	有色金属工业人才中心		

职通中文
Access to Vocational Chinese

电梯安装与维修保养

Elevator Installation and Maintenance

郁云峰 总主编
于天琪 陈维昌 副总主编
杭州职业技术学院 编

初级篇
Elementary

北京语言大学出版社
BEIJING LANGUAGE AND CULTURE
UNIVERSITY PRESS

©2025北京语言大学出版社，社图号24178

图书在版编目（CIP）数据

电梯安装与维修保养. 初级篇 / 郁云峰总主编；杭州职业技术学院编. -- 北京：北京语言大学出版社，2025.5. --（"职通中文"系列教材）. -- ISBN 978-7-5619-6657-0

Ⅰ．H195.4

中国国家版本馆CIP数据核字第2024NG0396号

电梯安装与维修保养（初级篇）
DIANTI ANZHUANG YU WEIXIU BAOYANG（CHUJIPIAN）

责任编辑：	王巧燕　赫栗
英文编辑：	侯晓娟
排版制作：	北京创艺涵文化发展有限公司
责任印制：	周　燚

出版发行：	北京语言大学出版社
社　　址：	北京市海淀区学院路15号，100083
网　　址：	www.blcup.com
电子信箱：	service@blcup.com
电　　话：	编 辑 部　8610-82303647/3592/3395
	国内发行　8610-82303650/3591/3648
	海外发行　8610-82303365/3080/3668
	北语书店　8610-82303653
	网购咨询　8610-82303908
印　　刷：	北京瑞禾彩色印刷有限公司

版　　次：	2025年5月第1版	**印　　次：**	2025年5月第1次印刷
开　　本：	787毫米×1092毫米　1/16	**印　　张：**	18.25
字　　数：	206千字		
定　　价：	115.00元		

PRINTED IN CHINA

凡有印装质量问题，本社负责调换。售后QQ号 1367565611，电话 010-82303590

前 言

为进一步推动各国学习者中文语言能力和专业技能深度融合，提升学习者围绕特定行业场景、典型工作任务使用中文进行沟通和交流的能力，持续满足中文学习者的职业规划和个人发展需求，实现优质教育资源共享，促进多彩文明交流互鉴，教育部中外语言交流合作中心联合有色金属工业人才中心，根据各国"中文+职业技能"教学发展实际需求，以中国职业院校为依托，组织职业教育、国际中文教育、出版和相关企业等领域的专家，共同研发"职通中文"系列教材及配套教学资源。

"职通中文"系列教材参照《国际中文教育中文水平等级标准》和《职业中文能力等级标准》，分为初、中、高三个等级。各等级均遵循"语言和技能相融合""好学、好教、好用"的编写理念，依据相关职业的典型工作场景、工作任务和高频用语，设计课文、会话、语言点和练习等板块，不断提升学习者在职业技术领域的中文应用水平和关键技术能力，为学习者尽快熟悉和适应工作环境提供帮助。本系列教材适用于在中国企业从事相关职业工作的各国员工，也适用于在华留学生或长短期培训人员，以及有意向了解中国语言文化和职业技能的学习者。

《电梯安装与维修保养（初级篇）》是"职通中文"系列教材之一，可用于中国"走出去"企业电梯维护保养岗位本土员工在岗语言和技术培训。通过学习本教材，学习者能够提升中文交际能力、技能操作水平，能够在从事的相关工作中与中国员工或客户用中文进行简单的工作交流，能够按照中文岗位说明书完成相应的工作内容，并掌握基本的电梯维保与检查的流程和操作技巧。

本教材共30课。通过深入中国民族电梯品牌西奥电梯等企业进行调研，编写组选取了30个典型工作任务和相应高频用语，融入中文语言使用习惯，设计了复习、热身、学习生词、学习课文、学习语法、汉字书写、职业拓展（文化拓展）和小结8大学习模块。在生词、课文、语法模块，强调语言学习复现率，设计了不同类型的测试练习。结合电梯维修保养过程中的常用短语和短句，配以相关资源，既能浸润语言学习环境，又能引导学习者反复观摩技能操作，从而帮助学习者达到基本沟通和技能习得的目的。

在本教材编写初期，考虑到其适用对象主要为"双零"基础的中国企业海外本土员工，编写组选取了较典型的工作任务框定了目录，并遵循"一课一技能点"的原则反复打磨课文，最后结合《国际中文教育中文水平等级标准》，按照"从前往后、先易后难"的原则挑选生词和语法。此外，还设计了丰富有趣的练习，进行内容的复现。为了帮助学习者更好地理解专业词语，教材配以大量的图片，并设计了常用的词语搭配和练习，以增强学习效果。

本教材由杭州职业技术学院特种设备学院郭伟刚（院长／教授）、潘国庆（骨干教师／高工）、刘博担任主编，付世州、翁海明、王玉云担任副主编，王正伟、陶宝春、王琳、崔富义、牟彦春、韩霁等参与编写。具体分工为：郭伟刚负责统稿工作，潘国庆、王正伟、翁海明、陶宝春负责从专业角度对课文进行编写和反复打磨，刘博、付世州负责根据国际中文教学标准和要求对语料进行加工，王琳负责翻译，西奥电梯王玉云负责落实教材在企业的试用和意见反馈。

本教材得到了各级领导和专家的指导和支持，崔永华、苏英霞、梁宇、宋继华、刘建国、梁赤民、陈曼倩等专家学者提出了许多宝贵建议，我们在此表示衷心感谢。教材还得益于教育部中外语言交流合作中心、有色金属工业人才中心、杭州职业技术学院和北京语言大学出版社的鼎力支持和精心指导，在此一并表示感谢。

"职通中文"系列教材的出版和应用能够促进各国"中文＋职业技能"人才的培养，推动当地经济发展，从而为构建人类命运共同体做出积极贡献。由于项目团队学识和相关经验有限，加之时间紧迫，本书肯定有许多疏漏、不足之处。恳请本书的使用者将发现的问题反馈给我们，以便我们在再版和编写相关教材时改进。

编写团队
2024年11月

Preface

In order to further promote the deep integration of Chinese language proficiency and professional skills among learners from various countries and enhance their ability to communicate and interact in Chinese in specific industry scenarios and typical work tasks, the Center for Language Education and Cooperation under the Ministry of Education, in collaboration with China Nonferrous Metal Industry Talent Center, has organized experts from vocational education, international Chinese education, publishing, and related enterprises to jointly develop the "Access to Vocational Chinese" series of textbooks and supporting teaching resources. Based on the actual needs of "Chinese + Vocational Skills" teaching development in various countries and relying on Chinese vocational colleges, the series aims to continuously meet the career planning and personal development needs of Chinese learners, realize the sharing of high-quality educational resources, and promote exchanges and mutual learning among diverse civilizations.

In reference to *Chinese Proficiency Grading Standards for International Chinese Language Education and Chinese Proficiency Standards for Vocational Education*, the "Access to Vocational Chinese" series of textbooks is divided into three levels: elementary, intermediate, and advanced. All the levels follow the writing philosophy of "integrating language and skills" and "being easy to learn, teach, and use." The textbooks are designed around typical work scenarios, work tasks, and high-frequency terms of relevant professions, with sections on texts, conversations, language points, and exercises, continuously improving learners' Chinese application skills and key technical abilities in the vocational and technical fields, providing assistance for learners to quickly familiarize themselves with and adapt to the work environment. This series of textbooks is suitable for international employees engaged in relevant professions in Chinese companies, international students or trainees in China, as well as learners interested in Chinese language, culture, and vocational skills.

Elevator Installation and Maintenance (Elementary Level) is a book in the "Access to Vocational Chinese" series. It can be used for the language and technical training of elevator maintenance personnel working in Chinese enterprises implementing the "going global" strategy. After learning this textbook, students can improve their Chinese communication skills and technical operation proficiency. They will be able to communicate in Chinese with Chinese employees or customers in related work, complete the corresponding work following the Chinese job descriptions, and master the basic elevator maintenance and inspection processes and operation skills.

This textbook is composed of 30 lessons. Through in-depth research on Xi'ao Elevator, a national elevator brand in China, and other enterprises, the writing team selected 30 typical work tasks and the corresponding frequently-used words, integrated Chinese language usage habits, and designed eight learning modules: revision, warm-up, words and expressions, text, grammar, writing Chinese characters, career insight (culture insight), and summary. In the words and expressions, text, and grammar modules, it emphasizes the repetition of language learning and designs quizzes and exercises of different types. Integrating the common phrases and short sentences in elevator maintenance process and providing the related resources not only help learners immerse themselves in the language learning environment, but also guide them to repeatedly observe the skills, thereby aiding them in achieving basic communication and acquiring skills.

In the early stage of writing this textbook, considering its target users are overseas employees of Chinese enterprises without previous Chinese language learning or skill learning experience, the writing team determined the table of contents based on the typical work tasks, and repeatedly revised the texts following the principle of "teaching one skill in one lesson". At last, new words and grammar are selected and introduced step by step based on *Chinese Proficiency Grading Standards for International Chinese Language Education*. Besides these, diverse and interesting exercises are designed to review the content. To help learners better understand professional terms, the textbook has a large number of pictures, and

Preface

features common word collocations and exercises to enhance learning effect.

The editors-in-chief of this book are Guo Weigang (Dean/Professor), Pan Guoqing (Backbone Teacher/Senior Engineer) and Liu Bo from the Institute of Special Equipment at Hangzhou Vocational and Technical College, with Fu Shizhou, Weng Haiming and Wang Yuyun serving as deputy editors-in-chief, and Wang Zhengwei, Tao Baochun, Wang Lin, Cui Fuyi, Mu Yanchun, and Han Ji participating in the writing. Guo Weigang is responsible for the overall content review, Pan Guoqing, Wang Zhengwei, Weng Haiming, and Tao Baochun are responsible for writing and revising the text in a professional way, Liu Bo and Fu Shizhou are responsible for corpus processing following the standards and requirements of teaching Chinese as a foreign language, Wang Lin is responsible for translation, and Wang Yuyun from Xi'ao Elevator is responsible for implementing the trial use and getting the feedback on the textbook from the enterprise.

This textbook has been developed with the guidance and support of leaders and professionals from various fields. We'd like to express our heartfelt thanks to Cui Yonghua, Su Yingxia, Liang Yu, Song Jihua, Liu Jianguo, Liang Chimin, Chen Manqian and other experts and scholars for their valuable suggestions. Thanks also go to the Center for Language Education and Cooperation of MOE, China Nonferrous Metals Industry Talent Center, Hangzhou Vocational and Technical College, and Beijing Language and Culture University Press for their support and guidance.

The publication and application of the "Access to Vocational Chinese" series of textbooks aim to develop talents with "Chinese + Vocational Skills" across the globe, promote local economies, and make positive contributions to building a community with a shared future. Due to limited knowledge and related experience of the project team, as well as time constraints, this book is bound to have many deficiencies that need improvement. We sincerely invite users of this book to provide feedback on any issues discovered, so that we can make improvements in future editions and related materials.

Compiling team,
November 2024

词类简称表
List of Abbreviations of Parts of Speech

词性 Part of speech	英译 English	简称 Abbreviation
名词 míngcí	noun	*n.*
专有名词 zhuānyǒu míngcí	proper noun	*pn.*
代词 dàicí	pronoun	*pron.*
数词 shùcí	numeral	*num.*
量词 liàngcí	measure word	*m.*
数量词 shùliàngcí	quantifier	*q.*
动词 dòngcí	verb	*v.*
能愿动词 néngyuàn dòngcí	optative	*opt.*
形容词 xíngróngcí	adjective	*adj.*
副词 fùcí	adverb	*adv.*
介词 jiècí	preposition	*prep.*
连词 liáncí	conjunction	*conj.*
助词 zhùcí	particle	*part.*
叹词 tàncí	interjection	*int.*
前缀 qiánzhuì	prefix	*pref.*
后缀 hòuzhuì	suffix	*suf.*
短语 duǎnyǔ	phrase	*phr.*

目 录 Contents

第 1 课	注意安全	Lesson 1	Be Safe 1
第 2 课	准备工作	Lesson 2	Get Ready 9
第 3 课	观察机房	Lesson 3	Observe the Machine Room ... 18
第 4 课	断开电源	Lesson 4	Disconnect the Power Supply .. 27
第 5 课	检查曳引机	Lesson 5	Inspect the Traction Machine .. 36
第 6 课	更换减速箱润滑油	Lesson 6	Replace the Lubricant in the Reduction Gearbox 46
第 7 课	盘车救援	Lesson 7	Rescue with a Handwheel 55
第 8 课	使用万用表	Lesson 8	Use the Multimeter 64
第 9 课	测试紧急电动运行	Lesson 9	Test the Emergency Power Operation (EPO) 73
第 10 课	检查控制柜元件	Lesson 10	Inspect the Control Cabinet Components 83
第 11 课	释放制动器机械能	Lesson 11	Release the Mechanical Energy of the Brake 92
第 12 课	检查制动器	Lesson 12	Inspect the Brake 101
第 13 课	测量制动器间隙	Lesson 13	Measure the Clearances of the Brake 110
第 14 课	进入轿厢	Lesson 14	Get into the Elevator Car 120
第 15 课	查看轿厢照明	Lesson 15	Inspect the Lighting of the Elevator Car 129
第 16 课	测试报警功能	Lesson 16	Test the Alarm Function 139
第 17 课	观察井道部件	Lesson 17	Observe the Components in the Hoistway 149

第 18 课	测试极限开关功能	Lesson 18	Test the Function of the Final Limit Switch 159
第 19 课	检查导轨	Lesson 19	Inspect the Guide Rails 169
第 20 课	检查钢丝绳	Lesson 20	Inspect the Steel Wire Rope . 178
第 21 课	进入轿顶	Lesson 21	Enter the Elevator Car Roof .. 187
第 22 课	验证检修状态	Lesson 22	Verify the Inspection Mode .. 197
第 23 课	检查对重	Lesson 23	Inspect the Counterweight .. 207
第 24 课	检查油杯	Lesson 24	Inspect the Oil Cup 216
第 25 课	检查导靴	Lesson 25	Inspect the Guide Shoes 225
第 26 课	退出轿顶	Lesson 26	Exit the Elevator Car Roof 234
第 27 课	测量平层精度	Lesson 27	Test the Landing Accuracy ... 243
第 28 课	检查光幕功能	Lesson 28	Inspect the Function of the Light Curtain 251
第 29 课	测量轿门间隙	Lesson 29	Measure the Elevator Car Door's Clearances 260
第 30 课	更换按钮	Lesson 30	Replace the Button 269

第 1 课 Lesson 1

Zhùyì ānquán
注意安全
Be Safe

 **热身 Warm-up**

看图选词，将对应的字母填在括号里。Look at the pictures and choose the words. Put the corresponding letters in the brackets.

A.

B.

C.

D.

E.

F.

1	绝缘鞋	juéyuánxié	insulating shoes	(　　)
2	注意安全	zhùyì ānquán	be safe, watch out	(　　)
3	电梯工	diàntīgōng	elevator worker	(　　)
4	电梯	diàntī	elevator	(　　)

| 5 | 安全帽 | ānquánmào | safety helmet | (　　) |
| 6 | 工作服 | gōngzuòfú | work clothes | (　　) |

学习生词 Words and Expressions 🎧 01-01

1	注意	zhù//yì	v.	pay attention to
2	安全	ānquán	n./adj.	safety; safe
3	我	wǒ	pron.	I, me
4	是	shì	v.	be
5	电梯工	diàntīgōng	n.	elevator worker
6	的	de	part.	used to express possession, or after an adjective to describe a noun
7	工作	gōngzuò	n./v.	job
8	维保	wéibǎo	v.	maintain
9	电梯	diàntī	n.	elevator
10	要	yào	opt.	need
11	穿	chuān	v.	wear, put on (clothes)
12	工作服	gōngzuòfú	n.	work clothes
13	绝缘鞋	juéyuánxié	n.	insulating shoes
14	戴	dài	v.	wear (a hat, gloves, etc.)
15	安全帽	ānquánmào	n.	safety helmet

第1课 | 注意安全

词语练习 Word Exercises

1. 认读词语。 Recognize and read the words.

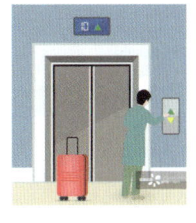  

电梯　　　　　　　电梯工　　　　　　　注意安全

安全帽　　　　　　工作服　　　　　　　绝缘鞋

2. 朗读词语搭配。 Read aloud the word collocations.

❶ 戴	戴安全帽	
❷ 穿	穿工作服	
	穿绝缘鞋	
❸ 维保	维保电梯	

3

 学习课文 Text 🎧 01-02

注意安全
Zhùyì ānquán

Wǒ shì diàntīgōng, wǒ de gōngzuò shì wéibǎo diàntī.
我是电梯工，我的工作是维保电梯。

Wéibǎo diàntī yào zhùyì ānquán, yào chuān gōngzuòfú, juéyuánxié,
维保电梯要注意安全，要穿工作服、绝缘鞋，

dài ānquánmào.
戴安全帽。

Be Safe

I am an elevator worker, and my job is to maintain elevators. To be safe, I need to wear work clothes, insulating shoes, and a safety helmet when working.

课文练习 Text Exercises

1. 判断对错。Tell whether the following statements are true (T) or false (F).

　① 电梯工要注意安全。　　　　　　　　　　　　　　(　　)
　② 电梯工的工作是维保电梯。　　　　　　　　　　　(　　)
　③ 电梯工要穿工作服。　　　　　　　　　　　　　　(　　)
　④ 电梯工要戴安全帽。　　　　　　　　　　　　　　(　　)

2. 选词填空。Choose the words to fill in the blanks.

For example：我穿（ B ）。　　A. 安全帽　　B. 绝缘鞋

① 我是（　　）工。　　　　A. 电梯　　　B. 安全

② 电梯工要穿（　　）。　　A. 绝缘鞋　　B. 安全帽

③ 我的工作是（　　）电梯。A. 维保　　　B. 注意

④ 电梯工要戴（　　）。　　A. 安全帽　　B. 工作服

学习语法 Grammar

语法点 1 Grammar Point 1

"是"字句　"是" Sentence

"是" indicates the similarity or category of something. A "是" sentence usually goes like "A 是 B" (A is B) or "A 不是 B" (A is not B). For example,

例句			英文翻译
Subject	是 / 不是	Object	
Wǒ 我	shì 是	diàntīgōng. 电梯工。	I'm an elevator worker.
Wǒ de gōngzuò 我 的 工作	shì 是	wéibǎo diàntī. 维保 电梯。	My job is to maintain elevators.
Zhè 这	bú shì 不是	ānquánmào. 安全帽。	This is not a safety helmet.

连词成句。Rearrange the words into sentences.

For example：①安全帽　②是　③这（this）→ ③＿＿＿＿＿②＿＿＿＿＿①

① ①电梯工　②是　③我→＿＿＿＿＿＿＿＿＿＿＿＿＿＿＿

② ①我　②老师（teacher）　③是→＿＿＿＿＿＿＿＿＿＿＿＿＿

3. ①绝缘鞋　②这　③是→ _____

4. ①我　②是　③不　④中国人（Chinese）→ _____

语法点 2 Grammar Point 2

能愿动词"要" The Optative Verb "要"

"要" is used before a verb to indicate the need to do something. For example,

例句			英文翻译
Sb./Sth.	要	VP	
Wéibǎo diàntī 维保 电梯	yào 要	zhùyì ānquán. 注意 安全。	Be safe when maintaining elevators.
Diàntīgōng 电梯工	yào 要	chuān gōngzuòfú. 穿 工作服。	Elevator workers need to wear work clothes.
Diàntīgōng 电梯工	yào 要	dài ānquánmào. 戴 安全帽。	Elevator workers need to wear safety helmets.

选词填空。Choose the words to fill in the blanks.

1. 电梯工_____穿绝缘鞋。　　A. 是　　B. 要
2. 我_____戴安全帽。　　A. 是　　B. 要
3. 我_____穿工作服。　　A. 是　　B. 要
4. 电梯工_____维保电梯。　　A. 是　　B. 要

汉字书写 Writing Chinese Characters

第1课 注意安全

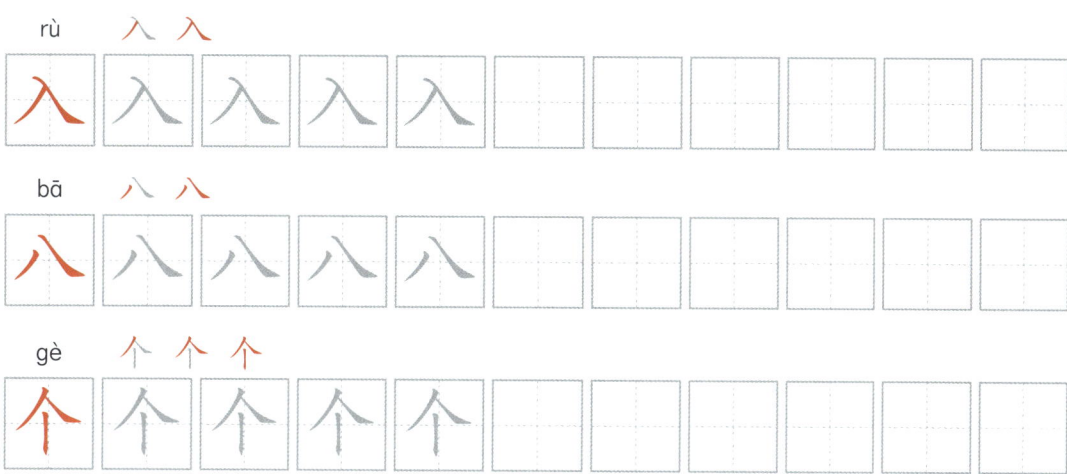

 **职业拓展** Career Insight

辘轳 Windlass

Windlass is the world's earliest water-lifting device invented by Chinese people. Similar to the modern elevator, a windlass consists of a headgear, a frame, a bucket and a handle. The

mechanical use of a shaft and a wheel ingeniously enables people to lift buckets full of water. It was as early as the Zhou Dynasty that the first windlass appeared, and its heyday was the Spring and Autumn Period and the Warring States Period. In addition to irrigation, windlasses were widely used in mining and house building. It stands as a testament to the infinite wisdom and creative ingenuity of ancient Chinese.

7

 小结 Summary

词语 Words

朗读下列词语。Read aloud the following words.

电梯工	安全帽	电梯	绝缘鞋
维保	工作	是	要
我	安全		

语法 Grammar

朗读下列句子。Read aloud the following sentences.

1. 我是电梯工。
2. 我的工作是维保电梯。
3. 维保电梯要注意安全。
4. 电梯工要戴安全帽。

课文理解 Text Comprehension

复述课文内容。Retell the text.

1. 我是……，我的工作是……。
2. 维保电梯要……，要穿……、……，戴……。

第 2 课 Lesson 2

准备工作 Zhǔnbèi gōngzuò
Get Ready

 复习 Revision

根据图片选择词语。Choose the words based on the pictures.

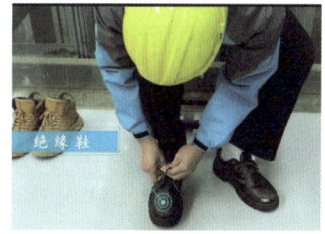

① 穿绝缘鞋（　　）
　戴绝缘鞋（　　）

② 穿工作服（　　）
　戴工作服（　　）

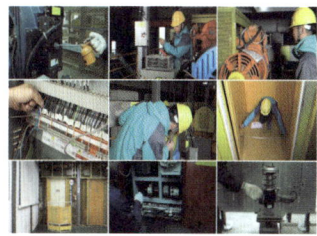

③ 注意电梯（　　）
　维保电梯（　　）

④ 戴安全帽（　　）
　穿安全帽（　　）

9

热身 Warm-up

看图选词，将对应的字母填在括号里。Look at the pictures and choose the words. Put the corresponding letters in the brackets.

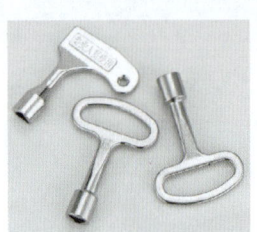

A.

B.

C.

D.

E.

F.

1	层门	céngmén	landing door	( )
2	工具	gōngjù	tool	( )
3	三角钥匙	sānjiǎo yàoshi	triangle key	( )
4	护栏	hùlán	guard rail	( )
5	轿厢	jiàoxiāng	elevator car	( )
6	顶门器	dǐngménqì	door stopper	( )

第 2 课 | 准备工作

 ## 学习生词 Words and Expressions 🎧 02-01

1	准备	zhǔnbèi	*v.*	prepare
2	前	qián	*n.*	before
3	工具	gōngjù	*n.*	tool
4	为了	wèile	*prep.*	for, to
5	层门	céngmén	*n.*	landing door
6	外面	wàimiàn	*n.*	outside
7	和	hé	*conj.*	and
8	轿厢	jiàoxiāng	*n.*	elevator car
9	里面	lǐmiàn	*n.*	in, inside
10	放	fàng	*v.*	put, place
11	护栏	hùlán	*n.*	guard rail
12	三角钥匙	sānjiǎo yàoshi	*phr.*	triangle key
13	顶门器	dǐngménqì	*n.*	door stopper
14	用	yòng	*prep.*	with, by means of
15	打开	dǎ//kāi	*v.*	open
16	阻止	zǔzhǐ	*v.*	prevent
17	关闭	guānbì	*v.*	close

11

词语练习 Word Exercises

1. 认读词语。Recognize and read the words.

护栏

轿厢

工具

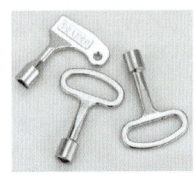
三角钥匙

顶门器

层门

2. 看图连线，并朗读词语搭配。Look at the pictures and match the words. Then read aloud the word collocations.

❶ 层门   里面

❷ 轿厢   外面

❸ 关闭   护栏

❹ 放   层门

第 2 课 | 准备工作

 **学习课文 Text** 🎧 02-02

准备 工作 Zhǔnbèi gōngzuò

工作前要准备工具。为了安全，层门外面和轿厢里面要放护栏。准备三角钥匙和顶门器，用三角钥匙打开层门，用顶门器阻止层门关闭。

Get Ready

Prepare tools before work. For safety, put a guard rail outside the landing door and inside the elevator car. Prepare a triangle key and a door stopper. Use the triangle key to open the landing door and use the stopper to prevent the door from closing.

课文练习 Text Exercises

1. 判断对错。Tell whether the following statements are true (T) or false (F).

   1. 工作前要准备工具。　　　　　　　　　　　　　　（　　）
   2. 轿厢里面要放护栏。　　　　　　　　　　　　　　（　　）

13

③ 层门外面要放护栏。　　　　　　　　　　（　　）

④ 用顶门器阻止层门打开。　　　　　　　　（　　）

2. 选词填空。Choose the words to fill in the blanks.

① 工作前要（　　）护栏。　　A. 准备　　　B. 打开

② 用三角钥匙打开（　　）。　A. 轿厢　　　B. 层门

③ 层门外面要放（　　）。　　A. 护栏　　　B. 顶门器

④ 用顶门器阻止层门（　　）。A. 关闭　　　B. 工作

学习语法 Grammar

语法点1 Grammar Point 1

……前

" 前 " is an adverbial in a Chinese sentence, indicating that something happens before another event or a point in time. For example,

例句	英文翻译
Gōngzuò qián yào zhǔnbèi gōngjù. 工作 前要准备工具。	Prepare tools before work.
Gōngzuò qián yào chuān gōngzuòfú. 工作 前要 穿 工作服。	Wear work clothes before work.
Wéibǎo diàntī qián yào fàng hùlán. 维保 电梯 前 要 放 护栏。	Place a guard rail before maintaining the elevator.

连词成句。Rearrange the words into sentences.

① ①要　②工作服　③前　④工作　⑤穿

　→ _____

第 2 课 | 准备工作

2 ①准备　②前　③工作　④工具　⑤要
→ _____

3 ①前　②电梯　③放　④要　⑤护栏　⑥维保
→ _____

4 ①层门　②前　③打开　④准备　⑤要　⑥顶门器
→ _____

语法点 2　Grammar Point 2

为了……

"为了" indicates the purpose of an action. In a Chinese sentence, "为了" is usually used before the action. For example,

例句	英文翻译
Wèile ānquán, yào dài ānquánmào. 为了安全，要戴安全帽。	Wear a helmet for safety reasons.
Wèile dǎkāi céngmén, yào zhǔnbèi sānjiǎo yàoshi. 为了打开层门，要准备三角钥匙。	Prepare a triangle key to open the landing door.
Wèile zǔzhǐ céngmén guānbì, yào zhǔnbèi dǐngménqì. 为了阻止层门关闭，要准备顶门器。	Prepare a door stopper to prevent the landing door from closing.

句子连线。Match the sentences.

1 为了安全，　　　　　　　要准备三角钥匙。

2 为了打开层门，　　　　　要戴安全帽。

3 为了阻止层门关闭，　　　要学习中文（Chinese）。

4 为了工作，　　　　　　　要准备顶门器。

 ## 汉字书写 Writing Chinese Characters

 ## 文化拓展 Culture Insight

造纸术 Papermaking

Turning plant fiber into paper is an epoch-making invention of Chinese people. Papermaking accelerated the spread of culture and knowledge—it became much easier to record words and pictures. The earliest linen paper appeared in the Western Han Dynasty. This technology was later improved by Cai Lun in the Eastern Han Dynasty. With the passage of time and the emergence of a large number of new materials and tools, the types of paper have proliferated into a rich diversity. This extraordinary art even crossed the oceans and had a far-reaching impact on the evolution of world civilization.

第 2 课 | 准备工作

 **小结 Summary**

 词语 Words

朗读下列词语。Read aloud the following words.

轿厢	护栏	三角钥匙	顶门器
层门	外面	和	打开
里面	放		

语法 Grammar

朗读下列句子。Read aloud the following sentences.

1. 工作前，要准备工具。
2. 工作前，要穿工作服。
3. 为了安全，层门外面要放护栏。
4. 为了安全，轿厢里面要放护栏。

课文理解 Text Comprehension

复述课文内容。Retell the text.

1. 工作前要准备……。
2. 为了……，层门……和轿厢……要放……。
3. 准备……和……。
4. ……打开层门，……阻止层门关闭。

17

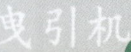

第 3 课 Lesson 3

Guānchá jīfáng
观察机房
Observe the Machine Room

复习 Revision

根据图片选择词语。Choose the words based on the pictures.

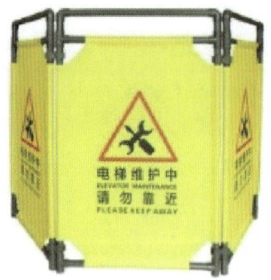

❶ 层门（   ）
　护栏（   ）

❷ 工具（   ）
　三角钥匙（   ）

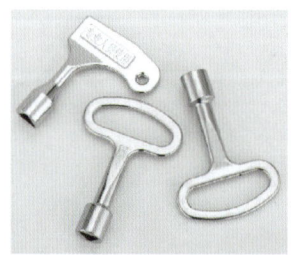

❸ 三角钥匙（   ）
　顶门器（   ）

❹ 轿厢（   ）
　工作（   ）

第 3 课 | 观察机房

热身 Warm-up

看图连线。Look at the pictures and match them with the words.

zhìdòngqì	yèyǐnlún	yèyǐnjī	jīfáng	xiànsùqì
制动器	曳引轮	曳引机	机房	限速器
brake	traction sheave	traction machine	machine room	speed limiter

学习生词 Words and Expressions 🎧 03-01

1	观察	guānchá	v.	observe
2	机房	jīfáng	n.	machine room
3	这	zhè	pron.	this
4	有	yǒu	v.	have, there be
5	电源盒	diànyuánhé	n.	power box
6	曳引机	yèyǐnjī	n.	traction machine
7	控制柜	kòngzhìguì	n.	control cabinet
8	限速器	xiànsùqì	n.	speed limiter
9	盘车手轮	pánchē shǒulún	phr.	handwheel

19

10	松闸扳手	sōngzhá bānshou	*phr.*	brake release wrench
11	由	yóu	*prep.*	by
12	电动机	diàndòngjī	*n.*	motor
13	制动器	zhìdòngqì	*n.*	brake
14	曳引轮	yèyǐnlún	*n.*	traction sheave
15	组成	zǔchéng	*v.*	consist

 词语练习 **Word Exercises**

1. 认读词语。Recognize and read the words.

   曳引轮   松闸扳手   限速器

 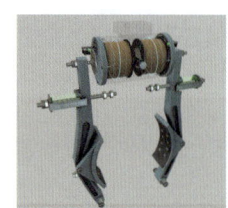 

   曳引机   制动器   盘车手轮

2. 朗读词语搭配。Read aloud the word collocations.

❶ 电源盒	打开电源盒	

第 3 课 | 观察机房

❷ 控制柜	打开控制柜	
❸ 观察	观察曳引机	
	观察机房	

学习课文 Text 🎧 03-02

观察 机房
Guānchá jīfáng

这是电梯机房。机房里面有电源盒、曳引机、控制柜、限速器、盘车手轮、松闸扳手。曳引机由电动机、制动器、曳引轮组成。

Observe the Machine Room

This is an elevator machine room. There is a power box, a traction machine, a control cabinet, a speed limiter, a handwheel, and a brake release wrench. The traction machine consists of a motor, a brake and a traction sheave.

课文练习 Text Exercises

1. 判断对错。Tell whether the following statements are true (T) or false (F).

   ① 机房里面有电源盒和限速器。　　　　　　　　　　（　　）
   ② 机房里面有曳引机和控制柜。　　　　　　　　　　（　　）
   ③ 曳引机由电动机、制动器、控制柜组成。　　　　　（　　）
   ④ 机房里面有盘车手轮和护栏。　　　　　　　　　　（　　）

2. 选词填空。Choose the words to fill in the blanks.

   ① 观察机房，机房里面有（　　　）。
      A. 安全帽　　　　　　B. 轿厢　　　　　　C. 限速器
   ② 机房里面没有（　　　）。
      A. 曳引机　　　　　　B. 控制柜　　　　　C. 层门
   ③ 机房里面有（　　　）。
      A. 层门　　　　　　　B. 电动机　　　　　C. 护栏
   ④ 曳引机由电动机、（　　　）、制动器组成。
      A. 限速器　　　　　　B. 电源盒　　　　　C. 曳引轮

第 3 课 | 观察机房

学习语法 Grammar

 语法点 1　Grammar Point 1

"有"字句　"有" Sentence

The verb "有" can be used in an existential sentence to indicate that somebody or something exists somewhere. For example,

例句			英文翻译
Subject	有	Object	
Jīfáng lǐmiàn 机房 里面	yǒu 有	yèyǐnjī. 曳引机。	There is a traction machine in the machine room.
Jīfáng lǐmiàn 机房 里面	yǒu 有	xiànsùqì. 限速器。	There is a speed limiter in the machine room.
Jiàoxiāng lǐmiàn 轿厢 里面	yǒu 有	hùlán. 护栏。	There is a guard rail in the elevator car.

连词成句。Rearrange the words into sentences.

1　①曳引机　②有　③机房　④里面　⑤和　⑥限速器
　→ _____

2　①电梯工　②机房　③里面　④有　⑤一个
　→ _____

3　①机房　②一个　③有　④里面　⑤安全帽
　→ _____

4　①轿厢　②里面　③有　④护栏
　→ _____

语法点 2 Grammar Point 2

由……组成

"由……组成" is a phrase indicating that something is composed of some parts or elements. For example,

		例句		英文翻译
Subject	由	Nominal phrase	组成	
Yèyǐnjī 曳引机	yóu 由	diàndòngjī、zhìdòngqì、yèyǐnlún 电动机、制动器、曳引轮	zǔchéng. 组成。	The traction machine consists of a motor, a brake and a traction sheave.
Diàntīmén 电梯门	yóu 由	céngmén hé jiàomén 层门 和 轿门	zǔchéng. 组成。	The elevator door consists of a landing door and a car door.
Wǒ de jiā 我的家	yóu 由	3 gè rén 3 个 人	zǔchéng. 组成。	My family consists of three people.

选词填空。Choose the words to fill in the blanks.

1. 机房里面_____曳引机和控制柜。 A. 有 B. 由
2. 曳引机_____电动机、制动器、曳引轮组成。 A. 有 B. 由
3. 机房里面_____一个限速器。 A. 有 B. 由
4. 机房里面_____盘车手轮和松闸扳手。 A. 有 B. 由

 **汉字书写 Writing Chinese Characters**

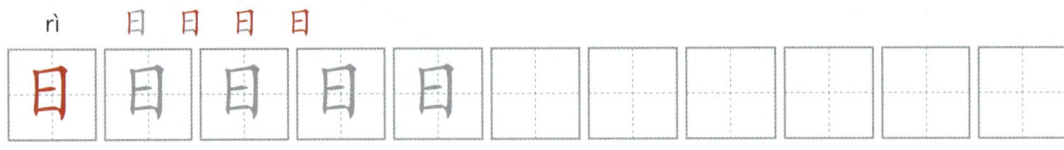

rì 日

职业拓展 Career Insight

安全升降梯的发明 The Invention of the Safety Elevator

Elisha Graves Otis, the first practitioner of elevator safety, was a legendary figure at the Exhibition of the Industry of All Nations held at the Crystal Palace in New York. He showed the audience his invention—a lifting apparatus, and he was very confident about its safety. He stood on it. Tension was building up as he was elevated high by an assistant. The assistant suddenly cut the cable. As shocked cries echoed around, the elevator came to a poised halt in mid-air—thanks to the safety device Otis had invented. "All safe, ladies and gentlemen, all safe," he said, waving to the crowd on the ground. What a great man! Otis became an overnight sensation for his new device and thus unveiled a new era for vertical mobility in human society.

 小结 Summary

 词语 Words

朗读下列词语。Read aloud the following words.

电源盒	松闸扳手	机房	观察
有	制动器	曳引机	控制柜
盘车手轮	这		

语法 Grammar

朗读下列句子。Read aloud the following sentences.

1. 机房里面有电源盒。
2. 机房里面有限速器。
3. 曳引机由电动机、制动器、曳引轮组成。
4. 电梯门由层门和轿门组成。

课文理解 Text Comprehension

复述课文内容。Retell the text.

1. 这是……。
2. 机房里面有……、……、……、限速器、盘车手轮、松闸扳手。
3. 曳引机由……、……、……组成。

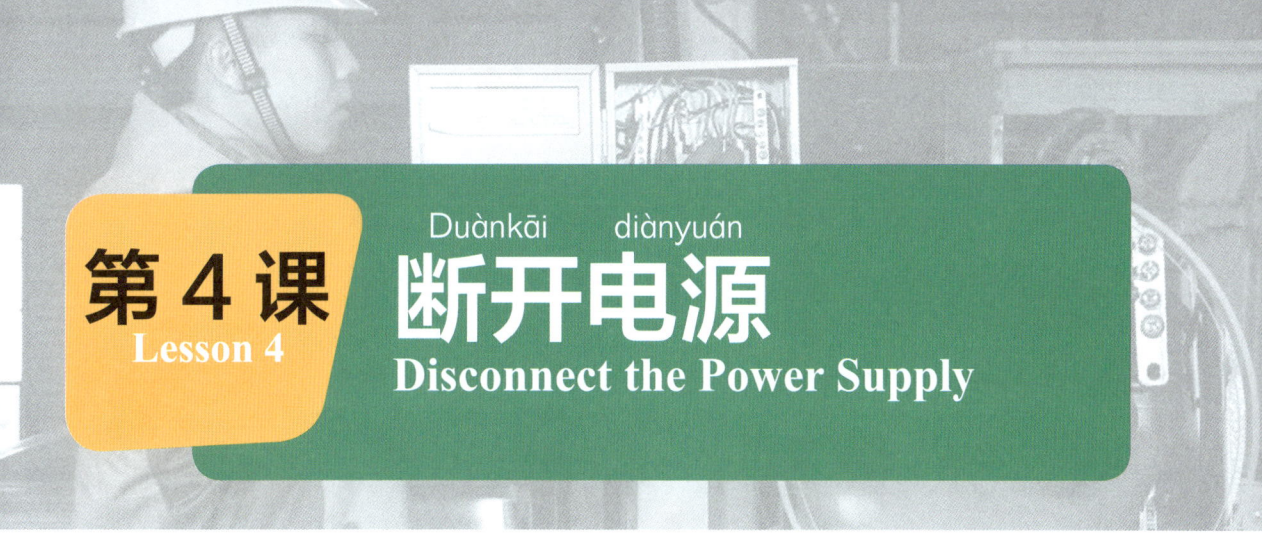

第 4 课 Lesson 4
Duànkāi diànyuán
断开电源
Disconnect the Power Supply

 复习 Revision

根据图片选择词语。Choose the words based on the pictures.

　　1 制动器（　　）
　　　　　曳引机（　　）

　　2 控制柜（　　）
　　　　　电源盒（　　）

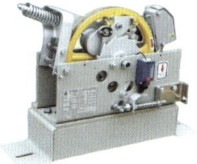　　3 限速器（　　）
　　　　　电源盒（　　）

　　4 机房（　　）
　　　　　层门（　　）

　　5 控制柜（　　）
　　　　　制动器（　　）

　　6 曳引轮（　　）
　　　　　限速器（　　）

27

热身 Warm-up

看图连线。Look at the pictures and match them with the words.

  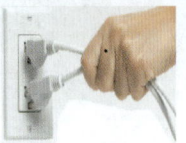  

biāopái	duànkāi	suǒ	kōngqì kāiguān	jiǎnxiū kāiguān
标牌	断开	锁	空气 开关	检修 开关
sign	disconnect	lock	air switch	inspection switch

学习生词 Words and Expressions 04-01

1	断开	duànkāi	*phr.*	disconnect
2	电源	diànyuán	*n.*	power supply
3	先	xiān	*adv.*	first
4	把	bǎ	*prep.*	used to put the object before the verb
5	好	hǎo	*adj.*	well
6	再	zài	*adv.*	then
7	到	dào	*v.*	to
8	然后	ránhòu	*conj.*	then

第 4 课 | 断开电源

9	旋转	xuánzhuǎn	*v.*	rotate
10	检修开关	jiǎnxiū kāiguān	*phr.*	inspection switch
11	转换	zhuǎnhuàn	*v.*	change
12	检修状态	jiǎnxiū zhuàngtài	*phr.*	inspection (a machine status or mode)
13	空气开关	kōngqì kāiguān	*phr.*	air switch
14	挂上	guàshang	*phr.*	put up
15	标牌	biāopái	*n.*	sign
16	锁	suǒ	*v./n.*	lock

 词语练习 Word Exercises

1. 认读词语。Recognize and read the words.

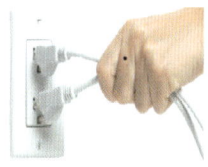

断开

锁

电源

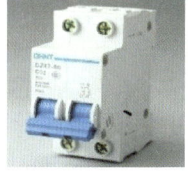

空气开关

标牌

检修开关

2. 朗读词语搭配。Read aloud the word collocations.

❶ 断开	断开电源	
❷ 电源盒	关闭电源盒	
❸ 标牌	挂上标牌	
❹ 锁	锁上电源盒	

学习课文 Text 🎧 04-02

Duànkāi diànyuán
断开 电源

Xiān bǎ hùlán fànghǎo, zài dào jīfáng, ránhòu xuánzhuǎn
先 把 护栏 放好，再 到 机房，然后 旋转
jiǎnxiū kāiguān, bǎ diàntī zhuǎnhuàn dào jiǎnxiū zhuàngtài. Dǎkāi
检修开关，把 电梯 转换 到 检修 状态。打开
diànyuánhé, duànkāi kōngqì kāiguān. Guānbì diànyuánhé, guàshang
电源盒，断开 空气开关。关闭 电源盒，挂上
biāopái, ránhòu suǒshang diànyuánhé.
标牌，然后 锁上 电源盒。

第 4 课 | 断开电源

Disconnect the Power Supply

Put the guard rail in place first. Go to the machine room, and then rotate the inspection switch to change the elevator into an "Inspection" mode. Open the power box and disconnect the air switch. Close the power box, put up the sign, and then lock the power box.

课文练习 Text Exercises

1. 选择正确的顺序。Choose the right order.

   ① 旋转检修开关　　② 放护栏　　③ 转换到检修状态
   ④ 锁上电源盒　　　⑤ 挂上标牌　⑥ 到机房
   ⑦ 关闭电源盒　　　⑧ 断开空气开关　⑨ 打开电源盒

   A. ①②③④⑤⑥⑦⑧⑨　　　　B. ②⑥①③⑨⑧⑦⑤④
   C. ⑧③⑦①⑤④⑨②⑥

   正确的顺序为（　　）。
   The correct order is (　　)。

2. 选词填空。Choose the words and fill in the blanks.

   ① 旋转（　　）后，再断开空气开关。　　A. 检修开关　　B. 盘车手轮
   ② 断开电源前，要放（　　）。　　　　　A. 护栏　　　　B. 标牌
   ③ 空气开关在电源盒（　　）。　　　　　A. 里面　　　　B. 外面
   ④ 关闭电源盒，挂上（　　）。　　　　　A. 检修开关　　B. 标牌

学习语法 Grammar

语法点 1 Grammar Point 1

先……，再……

"先……，再……" indicates taking two actions in succession, emphasizing that the latter must come after the former. For example,

例句	英文翻译
Xiān dào jīfáng, zài xuánzhuǎn jiǎnxiū kāiguān. 先到机房，再旋转检修开关。	Go to the machine room first, and then rotate the inspection switch.
Xiān guānbì diànyuánhé, zài guàshang biāopái. 先关闭电源盒，再挂上标牌。	Close the power box first, and then put up the sign.
Xiān chuān gōngzuòfú, zài wéibǎo diàntī. 先穿工作服，再维保电梯。	Put on your work clothes first, and then maintain the elevator.

改写句子。Rewrite the sentences.

1. 先准备工具，然后维保电梯。

    先_____，再_____。

2. 挂上标牌前，先关闭电源盒。

    先_____，再_____。

3. 到机房前，先放护栏。

    先_____，再_____。

4. 断开电源，然后维保电梯。

    先_____，再_____。

语法点 2 Grammar Point 2

"把"字句 "把" Sentence

"把" indicates doing something and changing the position or state of somebody or something. A "把" sentence usually goes like "subject + 把 + object + phrasal verb". A negative adverb or auxiliary verb can be placed before "把". For example,

例句			英文翻译
把	Object	Phrasal verb	
Bǎ 把	hùlán 护栏	fànghǎo. 放好。	Put the guard rail in place.
Bǎ 把	diàntī 电梯	zhuǎnhuàn dào jiǎnxiū zhuàngtài. 转换 到 检修 状态。	Switch the elevator to the "Inspection" mode.
Bǎ 把	biāopái 标牌	guàshang. 挂上。	Put up the sign.

连词成句。Rearrange the words into sentences.

1 ①护栏　②好　③把　④放→ _____

2 ①把　②打开　③层门→ _____

3 ①安全帽　②上　③把　④戴→ _____

4 ①工具　②把　③准备　④好→ _____

 汉字书写 Writing Chinese Characters

shàng 上　上　上　上
上　上　上　上　上

xià 下　下　下
下　下　下　下　下

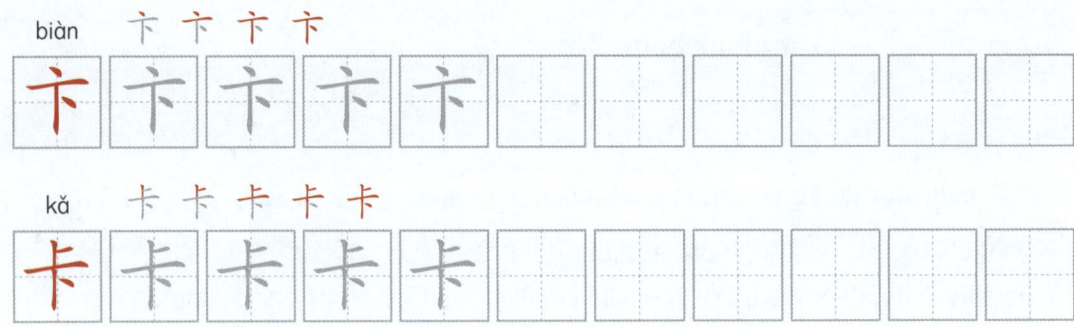

 文化拓展 Culture Insight

指南针 Compass

The magnetic needle on an axis is the major component of a compass, or *sinan* in ancient China. Under the influence of the Earth's natural magnetic field, the needle can freely rotate and keep its direction tangent to magnetic meridian, with its south pole pointing to the geographic south pole (which corresponds to the magnetic north pole). We are able to find directions thanks to this

feature. It is very useful in navigation, geodesy, traveling, military actions, etc. As one of the Four Great Inventions in ancient China, compass reflects Chinese people's gradual understanding of magnetism over a long period of time. It has had an immeasurable impact on human science and civilization.

第 4 课 | 断开电源

 小结 Summary

词语 Words

朗读下列词语。Read aloud the following words.

检修状态	检修开关	先	再
到	然后	旋转	挂上
把	断开		

语法 Grammar

朗读下列句子。Read aloud the following sentences.

❶ 先放护栏，再旋转检修开关。
❷ 先挂上标牌，再锁上电源盒。
❸ 把护栏放好。
❹ 把电梯转换到检修状态。

课文理解 Text Comprehension

复述课文内容。Retell the text.

❶ 先……，再到……，然后旋转……，把电梯……到……。
❷ 打开……，断开……。
❸ ……电源盒，挂上……，然后……电源盒。

第 5 课 Lesson 5

检查曳引机 Jiǎnchá yèyǐnjī
Inspect the Traction Machine

 **复习 Revision**

根据图片选择词语。Choose the words based on the pictures.

❶ 关闭电源盒（　　） ❷ 断开电源（　　）
　锁上电源盒（　　） 　旋转开关（　　）

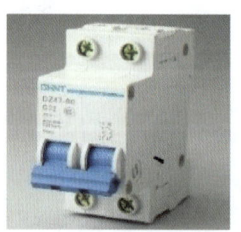 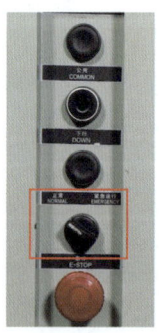

❸ 空气开关（　　） ❹ 检修开关（　　）
　电源盒（　　） 　曳引机（　　）

第 5 课 | 检查曳引机

 **热身 Warm-up**

看图连线。Look at the pictures and match them with the words.

  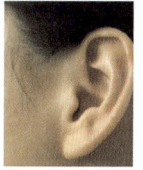  

ěrduo	kàn	tīng	yǎnjing	shēngyīn
耳朵	看	听	眼睛	声音
ear	see	hear	eye	sound

 **学习生词 Words and Expressions**  05-01

1	检查	jiǎnchá	v.	inspect, check
2	在	zài	prep.	in (on, at, etc.)
3	转动	zhuàndòng	v.	rotate
4	时	shí	n.	when
5	耳朵	ěrduo	n.	ear
6	听	tīng	v.	hear
7	声音	shēngyīn	n.	sound
8	很	hěn	adv.	very

9	大	dà	adj.	loud
10	说明	shuōmíng	v.	show, prove
11	故障	gùzhàng	n.	breakdown
12	眼睛	yǎnjing	n.	eye
13	看	kàn	v.	see
14	振动	zhèndòng	v.	vibrate
15	都	dōu	adv.	all, both

 词语练习　Word Exercises

1. 认读词语。Recognize and read the words.

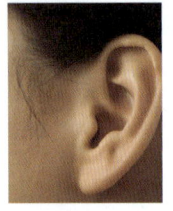　　　　　　　　　　

　　耳朵　　　　　　　听　　　　　　　声音

　　眼睛　　　　　　　看　　　　　　　故障

第 5 课 | 检查曳引机

2. 朗读词语搭配。Read aloud the word collocations.

❶ 检查	检查曳引机	
❷ 声音	声音很大	
❸ 听	听声音	
❹ 故障	曳引机故障	

学习课文 Text 05-02

检查 曳引机
Jiǎnchá yèyǐnjī

Zài jīfáng lǐmiàn, diàntīgōng jiǎnchá yèyǐnjī. Yèyǐnlún
在 机房 里面，电梯工 检查 曳引机。曳引轮

zhuàndòng shí, yòng ěrduo tīng shēngyīn, tīngdào shēngyīn hěn dà, shuōmíng
转动 时，用耳朵听 声音，听到 声音很大，说明

yǒu gùzhàng. Yòng yǎnjing kàn yèyǐnjī, kàndào yǒu zhèndòng, shuōmíng
有 故障。用眼睛看曳引机，看到有 振动，说明

yǒu gùzhàng. Yèyǐnjī yǒu zhèndòng、shēngyīn hěn dà, dōu shuōmíng
有 故障。曳引机有振动、声音 很大，都 说明

yǒu gùzhàng.
有 故障。

39

Inspect the Traction Machine

An elevator worker is inspecting the traction machine in the machine room. When the traction wheel is rotating, if the worker hears very loud sounds with his ears or sees vibrations with his eyes, both show break-downs of the machine.

课文练习 Text Exercises

1. 判断对错。Tell whether the following statements are true (T) or false (F).

   1. 检查曳引机要断开电源。　　　　　　　　　　　　　　　(　　)
   2. 检查曳引机要用眼睛看。　　　　　　　　　　　　　　　(　　)
   3. 曳引机有振动，说明有故障。　　　　　　　　　　　　　(　　)
   4. 曳引机声音很大，说明有故障。　　　　　　　　　　　　(　　)

2. 选词填空。Choose the words to fill in the blanks.

   1. 曳引机在机房（　　）检查。　　　A. 里面　　　B. 外面
   2. 用耳朵听（　　）。　　　　　　　A. 声音　　　B. 振动
   3. （　　）有振动，说明有故障。　　A. 控制柜　　B. 曳引机
   4. 用眼睛看曳引机，看到有（　　）。A. 声音　　　B. 振动

第 5 课 | 检查曳引机

学习语法 Grammar

 语法点 1 Grammar Point 1

用……

"用……" means doing something with a tool (or something else). For example,

例句	英文翻译
Diàntīgōng yòng ěrduo tīng shēngyīn. 电梯工 用耳朵听 声音。	The elevator worker hears sounds with (his) ears.
Wǒ yòng sānjiǎo yàoshi dǎkāi céngmén. 我 用 三角 钥匙 打开 层门。	I open the landing door with a triangle key.
Diàntīgōng yòng yǎnjing kàn yèyǐnjī. 电梯工 用 眼睛 看 曳引机。	The elevator worker sees the traction machine with (his) eyes.

连词成句。Rearrange the words into sentences.

1. ①曳引机 ②声音 ③听 ④耳朵 ⑤用 ⑥的

_____

2. ①眼睛 ②用 ③看 ④看到 ⑤振动 ⑥曳引机 ⑦有

_____

3. ①层门 ②阻止 ③顶门器 ④用 ⑤关闭

_____

4. ①维保 ②工具 ③我 ④用 ⑤电梯

_____

语法点 2 Grammar Point 2

范围、协同副词"都" The Adverb of Scope and Coordination "都"

The adverb "都" means all / both in Chinese. A sentence usually goes like "Subject + 都 + Verb Phrase". For example,

例句	英文翻译
Sānjiǎo yàoshi hé dǐngménqì dōu shì gōngjù. 三角钥匙和顶门器都是工具。	Both the triangle key and the door stopper are tools.
Yèyǐnjī shēngyīn dà、yǒu zhèndòng dōu shuōmíng yǒu gùzhàng. 曳引机声音大、有振动都说明有故障。	Both loud sounds and vibrations show breakdowns of the traction machine.
Yèyǐnjī hé xiànsùqì dōu zài jīfáng. 曳引机和限速器都在机房。	Both the traction machine and speed limiter are in the machine room.

改写句子。 Rewrite the sentences.

1. 我是电梯工。他是电梯工。
   _____和_____都_____。

2. 曳引机在机房。限速器在机房。
   _____和_____都_____。

3. 曳引机有故障。控制柜有故障。
   _____和_____都_____。

4. 他在轿厢外面。我在轿厢外面。
   _____和_____都_____。

第 5 课 | 检查曳引机

汉字书写 Writing Chinese Characters

dà
大 大 大 大
大 大 大 大 大

tài
太 太 太 太
太 太 太 太 太

tiān
天 天 天 天
天 天 天 天 天

fū
夫 夫 夫 夫
夫 夫 夫 夫 夫

职业拓展 Career Insight

无齿轮牵引机 Gearless Traction Machine

Gearless traction motor, an elevator without the gear reducer, uses a permanent magnet synchronous motor (PMSM) to drive the traction sheave. Otis Elevator Company introduced the world's first gearless traction elevator in 1903, and a new generation of PMSMs further improved its efficiency and performance in the 1990s. Today, gearless traction motors have become the mainstream choice in the market, and

have excellent performance in energy conservation, environmental protection, noise control, and space requirements for a machine room (even eliminating the need for a separate machine room). The appearance of gearless traction motors marks a breakthrough in elevator technology, indicating that elevator design has much room for improvement. To meet a variety of needs, they can ensure faster operation and greater load capacity in the future.

小结 Summary

词语 Words

朗读下列词语。Read aloud the following words.

在	声音	检查	眼睛
都	看	听	耳朵
时	用		

语法 Grammar

朗读下列句子。Read aloud the following sentences.

1. 用耳朵听曳引机的声音。
2. 用眼睛看曳引机，看到有振动。
3. 曳引机声音很大和有振动都说明有故障。
4. 曳引机和限速器都在机房。

课文理解 Text Comprehension

复述课文内容。Retell the text.

1. 在……里面，电梯工……。
2. 曳引轮……时，用……，听到……，说明……。
3. 用眼睛……，看到……，说明……。
4. ……、……，都说明有故障。

第 6 课 Lesson 6

Gēnghuàn jiǎnsùxiāng rùnhuáyóu
更换减速箱润滑油
Replace the Lubricant in the Reduction Gearbox

 复习 Revision

根据图片选择词语。Choose the words based on the pictures.

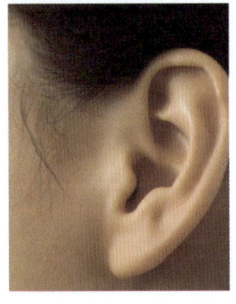

① 振动（　　）
　 耳朵（　　）

② 声音（　　）
　 故障（　　）

③ 看（　　）
　 听（　　）

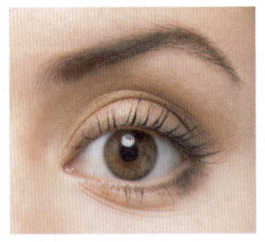

④ 机房（　　）
　 眼睛（　　）

第 6 课 | 更换减速箱润滑油

 **热身 Warm-up**

看图选词，将相应的字母填在括号里。Look at the pictures and choose the words. Put the corresponding letters in the brackets.

A. 　　　　　　　B. 　　　　　　　C.

D. 　　　　　　　E. 　　　　　　　F.

1	润滑油	rùnhuáyóu	lubricant	( )
2	油窗	yóuchuāng	oil window	( )
3	抹布	mābù	duster	( )
4	减速箱	jiǎnsùxiāng	reduction gearbox	( )
5	位置	wèizhì	position	( )
6	端盖	duāngài	cover	( )

学习生词 Words and Expressions 06-01

1	更换	gēnghuàn	v.	replace
2	减速箱	jiǎnsùxiāng	n.	reduction gearbox
3	润滑油	rùnhuáyóu	n.	lubricant
4	出油口	chūyóukǒu	n.	(oil) outlet
5	端盖	duāngài	n.	cover
6	旧	jiù	adj.	previous, old
7	抹布	mābù	n.	duster
8	擦	cā	v.	wipe
9	盖	gài	v.	put on (e.g. a cover)
10	注入	zhùrù	v.	pour into
11	新	xīn	adj.	new
12	油窗	yóuchuāng	n.	oil window
13	三分之二	sān fēn zhī èr	num.	two-thirds
14	位置	wèizhì	n.	position

第 6 课 | 更换减速箱润滑油

词语练习 Word Exercises

1. 认读词语。Recognize and read the words.

减速箱

润滑油

端盖

油窗

抹布

位置

2. 朗读词语搭配。Read aloud the word collocations.

❶ 端盖	打开端盖	
❷ 注入	注入润滑油	
❸ 擦	擦减速箱	
❹ 油窗	观察油窗	

学习课文 Text 🎧 06-02

更换减速箱润滑油
Gēnghuàn jiǎnsùxiāng rùnhuáyóu

更换润滑油前，先断开电源，再打开出油口端盖，把旧的润滑油放出来。用抹布擦出油口，盖上端盖。注入新的润滑油。观察油窗，润滑油要到减速箱三分之二的位置。

Replace the Lubricant in the Reduction Gearbox

Disconnect the power supply before replacing the lubricant. Then, open the cover of the oil outlet. Drain the previous lubricant. Wipe the outlet with a duster, put the cover back on, and then pour into the new lubricant. Observe the oil window and ensure that the lubricant reaches two-thirds of the reduction gearbox.

课文练习 Text Exercises

1. 判断对错。Tell whether the following statements are true (T) or false (F).

① 更换润滑油前，要先打开电源。　　　　　　　　　　（　　）

② 用抹布擦减速箱的出油口。 （　　）
③ 电梯工要放出新的润滑油。 （　　）
④ 新的润滑油要到减速箱三分之二的位置。 （　　）

2. 选词填空。Choose the words to fill in the blanks.

① 更换润滑油前，先（　　）电源。　　A. 断开　　B. 打开
② 盖上端盖前，用（　　）擦出油口。　　A. 抹布　　B. 电源
③ 更换润滑油时，要观察（　　）。　　A. 出油口　　B. 油窗
④ 放出旧的润滑油前，先打开（　　）。　　A. 端盖　　B. 电源

学习语法 Grammar

 语法点 1 Grammar Point 1

动词 + 上　V + "上"

"上" is used after a verb to indicate the completion of an action. For example,

例句	英文翻译
Dàishang ānquánmào. 戴上 安全帽。	Put on your safety helmet.
Guàshang biāopái. 挂上 标牌。	Put up the sign.
Gàishang duāngài. 盖上 端盖。	Put on the cover.

选词填空。Choose the words to fill in the blanks.

① 电梯工要穿（　　）工作服。　　A. 上　　B. 开
② 关闭电源盒，挂（　　）标牌。　　A. 上　　B. 开

3 盖（　　　）端盖。　　　　　　A. 上　　　　B. 开

4 维保电梯要戴（　　　）安全帽。　A. 上　　　　B. 开

语法点 2 Grammar Point 2

动词 + 出来　V + "出来"

"出来" is used after a verb to indicate the direction of an action. For example,

例句	英文翻译
Bǎ rùnhuáyóu fàng chulai. 把 润滑油 放 出来。	Drain the lubricant.
Bǎ hùlán ná chulai. 把 护栏 拿 出来。	Take out the guard rail.
Bǎ gōngjù ná chulai. 把 工具 拿 出来。	Take out the tools.

连词成句。Rearrange the words into sentences.

1 ①润滑油　②出来　③把　④放→ _____

2 ①拿　②把　③出来　④工作服 → _____

3 ①把　②拿　③护栏　④出来→ _____

4 ①出来　②拿　③把　④三角钥匙→ _____

 汉字书写 Writing Chinese Characters

sān　三 三 三
三　三　三　三　三

wáng　王 王 王 王
王　王　王　王　王

第 6 课 | 更换减速箱润滑油

yù
玉 玉 玉 玉 玉 玉
玉 玉 玉 玉 玉

zhǔ
主 主 主 主 主 主
主 主 主 主 主

 **文化拓展 Culture Insight**

长城 The Great Wall

The Great Wall has been a glorious legacy of China over the past 2,000 years. The earliest city walls can be traced back to the Spring and Autumn Period and the

Warring States Period, and were built to resist the invading nomadic peoples. After the first emperor of China, Qin Shihuang, unified China, the Great Wall underwent a series of expansions and repairs, and gradually formed its present grandeur.

The construction of the Great Wall was in its heyday in the Ming Dynasty, and most of the walls are relics of that period. The Great Wall is not only an architectural miracle in the history of military fortifications, but also a proof of Chinese people's wisdom and indomitable spirit. It is spectacular and majestic and attracts countless visitors from both home and abroad. The Great Wall is now a UNESCO World Heritage site. It witnesses the past glory of China and Chinese people's wish for peace and harmony.

 小结 Summary

词语 Words

朗读下列词语。Read aloud the following words.

端盖	油窗	减速箱	润滑油
更换	抹布	新	注入

语法 Grammar

朗读下列句子。Read aloud the following sentences.

1. 维保电梯前，把工具拿出来。
2. 打开端盖，把旧的润滑油放出来。
3. 用抹布擦出油口，再盖上端盖。
4. 挂上标牌。

课文理解 Text Comprehension

复述课文内容。Retell the text.

1. 更换润滑油前，先断开……，再打开出油口……，把……放出来。
2. 用……擦出油口，……端盖。
3. ……新的……。
4. 观察……，润滑油要到……的位置。

第 7 课 Lesson 7
Pánchē jiùyuán
盘车救援
Rescue with a Handwheel

 复习 Revision

根据图片选择词语。Choose the words based on the pictures.

1. 抹布（　　）
   工具（　　）

2. 减速箱（　　）
   限速器（　　）

3. 注入　（　　）
   润滑油（　　）

4. 端盖（　　）
   油窗（　　）

5. 减速箱（　　）
   油窗　（　　）

6. 位置（　　）
   出来（　　）

55

职通中文 电梯安装与维修保养（初级篇）

 ## 热身 Warm-up

看图连线。Look at the pictures and match them with the words.

    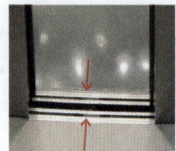

chéngkè	kùnrén	hǎn	píngcéng	jiùyuán
乘客	困人	喊	平层	救援
passenger	(sb.)be trapped	shout	landing floor	rescue

 ## 学习生词 Words and Expressions 🎧 07-01

1	救援	jiùyuán	v.	rescue
2	或者	huòzhě	conj.	or
3	困人	kùnrén	phr.	(sb.) be trapped
4	进行	jìnxíng	v.	(be) in progress
5	插入	chārù	phr.	insert
6	松开	sōngkāi	phr.	release
7	两	liǎng	num.	two
8	一起	yìqǐ	adv.	together
9	喊	hǎn	v.	shout

第 7 课 | 盘车救援

10	口号	kǒuhào	n.	slogan
11	同步	tóngbù	v.	synchronize
12	操作	cāozuò	v.	operate, work
13	移动	yídòng	v.	move
14	平层	píngcéng	n.	landing floor
15	乘客	chéngkè	n.	passenger
16	救	jiù	v.	rescue

 词语练习 Word Exercises

1. 认读词语。Recognize and read the words.

救援

盘车救援

平层

喊

乘客

困人

2. 朗读词语搭配。Read aloud the word collocations.

❶ 松开	松开制动器	
❷ 插入	插入盘车手轮	
	插入松闸扳手	
❸ 把乘客救出来		
❹ 同步操作		

学习课文 Text 🎧 07-02

Pánchē jiùyuán
盘车 救援

Diàntī yǒu gùzhàng huòzhě kùnrén shí, diàntīgōng yào jìnxíng
电梯 有 故障 或者 困人 时，电梯工 要 进行

第 7 课 | 盘车救援

盘车救援。断开电源,电梯工 A 插入盘车手轮,电梯工 B 插入松闸扳手,松开制动器。电梯工 A 旋转盘车手轮,两人一起喊口号,同步操作。移动轿厢到平层位置,把乘客救出来。

Rescue with a Handwheel

When the elevator breaks down or people are trapped, the elevator workers will rescue with a handwheel. After disconnecting power supply, elevator worker A inserts the handwheel, and elevator worker B inserts the brake release wrench to release the brake. Elevator worker A rotates the handwheel. Both of them shout slogans and work together to move the elevator car to the landing floor to rescue the passengers.

课文练习 Text Exercises

1. 判断对错。Tell whether the following statements are true (T) or false (F).

① 电梯困人时,要进行盘车救援。　　　　　　　　　　（　　）

② 救援时,先插入盘车手轮,然后断开电源。　　　　　（　　）

③ 旋转盘车手轮和松开制动器要同步操作。　　　　　（　　）

④ 移动轿厢到平层位置,然后把乘客救出来。　　　　（　　）

2. 选词填空。Choose the words to fill in the blanks.

1. 断开电源，电梯工插入（　　）。　　A. 三角钥匙　　B. 盘车手轮
2. 盘车手轮和松闸扳手要（　　）操作。　　A. 进行　　B. 同步
3. 电梯工 A 和电梯工 B 一起喊（　　）。　　A. 口号　　B. 乘客
4. 用松闸扳手（　　）制动器。　　A. 旋转　　B. 松开

学习语法 Grammar

语法点 1　Grammar Point 1

连词"或者"　The Conjunction "或者"

"或者（或）" indicates a selective relationship. A sentence usually goes like "或 A 或 B" or "A 或 B". "或" is mostly used in written Chinese. For example,

例句	英文翻译
Diàntī yǒu gùzhàng huòzhě kùnrén shí, yào jìnxíng pánchē jiùyuán. 电梯有故障或者困人时，要进行盘车救援。	When the elevator breaks down or people are trapped, the elevator worker will rescue with a handwheel.
Diàntīgōng A huòzhě diàntīgōng B fàng hùlán. 电梯工 A 或者电梯工 B 放护栏。	Elevator worker A or B will put the guard rail.
Wǒ huòzhě tā dǎkāi céngmén. 我或者他打开层门。	I or he will open the landing door.

选词填空。Choose the words to fill in the blanks.

1. 电梯困人（　　）有故障时，电梯工要进行盘车救援。　　A. 和　　B. 或者
2. 机房里面有曳引机（　　）控制柜。　　A. 和　　B. 或者
3. 维保电梯要穿工作服（　　）绝缘鞋。　　A. 和　　B. 或者
4. 我（　　）电梯工插入盘车手轮。　　A. 和　　B. 或者

第7课 | 盘车救援

语法点2 Grammar Point 2

……时

"……时" is an adverbial in a sentence, referring to a point in time or a period of time when something is happening. It's mostly used in written Chinese. It's equivalent to "当……的时候". For example,

例句	英文翻译
Diàntī kùnrén shí, diàntīgōng yào jìnxíng pánchē jiùyuán. 电梯困人时，电梯工要进行盘车救援。	When people in the elevator are trapped, the elevator worker will rescue with a handwheel.
Diàntī yǒu gùzhàng shí, diàntīgōng yào jìnxíng pánchē jiùyuán. 电梯有故障时，电梯工要进行盘车救援。	When the elevator breaks down, the elevator worker will rescue with a handwheel.
Jiàoxiāng dào píngcéng wèizhì shí, bǎ chéngkè jiù chūlái. 轿厢到平层位置时，把乘客救出来。	Passengers can be rescued when the elevator car reaches the landing floor.

连词成句。Rearrange the words into sentences.

1 ①安全　②注意　③工作　④要　⑤时
→ _____

2 ①工作　②穿　③时　④绝缘鞋　⑤要
→ _____

3 ①曳引机　②时　③转动　④声音　⑤要　⑥听
→ _____

4 ①盘车救援　②口号　③时　④喊　⑤一起　⑥要
→ _____

汉字书写 Writing Chinese Characters

职业拓展 Career Insight

无绳式电梯 Cordless Elevator

Cordless elevators entered the public eye at the beginning of the 21st century. Without a wire rope or a pulley, the cordless elevator runs with permanent magnet synchronous linear motor (PMSLM). Its characteristic is that the car is directly connected to the motor, and the movement of the car is controlled by adjusting the magnetic field. Cordless elevator is energy-saving, safe, high-performance and adaptable, and is considered as the future of elevator technology.

第 7 课 | 盘车救援

小结 Summary

词语 Words

朗读下列词语。Read aloud the following words.

插入	救援	移动	乘客
或者	进行	平层	松开
一起	操作		

语法 Grammar

朗读下列句子。Read aloud the following sentences.

1. 电梯工 A 或电梯工 B 插入盘车手轮。
2. 电梯工 A 或电梯工 B 插入松闸扳手。
3. 电梯困人时,电梯工要进行盘车救援。
4. 电梯有故障时,电梯工要进行盘车救援。

课文理解 Text Comprehension

复述课文内容。Retell the text.

1. 电梯有故障或者困人时,电梯工要进行……。
2. 断开电源,电梯工 A 插入……,电梯工 B 插入……,……制动器。
3. 电梯工 A 旋转……,两人一起喊……,同步……。
4. ……轿厢到……位置,把……救出来。

第 8 课 Lesson 8
Shǐyòng wànyòngbiǎo
使用万用表
Use the Multimeter

 复习 Revision

根据上一课课文选图填空。Choose the pictures to fill in the blanks based on the previous text.

　　A.　　　　　　　　B.　　　　　　　　C.

松开_____，旋转_____，把_____救出来。

 热身 Warm-up

看图连线。Look at the pictures and match them with the words.

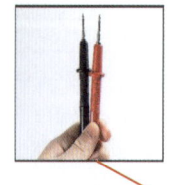　　　　

wànyòngbiǎo	biǎobǐ	chāzuò	shùzhí	xuánniǔ
万用表	表笔	插座	数值	旋钮
multimeter	probe, test pencil	socket	reading	knob

第 8 课 | 使用万用表

 ## 学习生词 Words and Expressions 08-01

1	使用	shǐyòng	v.	use
2	万用表	wànyòngbiǎo	n.	multimeter
3	红色	hóngsè	n.	red
4	表笔	biǎobǐ	n.	probe, test pencil
5	黑色	hēisè	n.	black
6	旋钮	xuánniǔ	n.	knob
7	选择	xuǎnzé	v.	select
8	蜂鸣	fēngmíng	n.	buzz
9	挡位	dǎngwèi	n.	voltage level, range
10	接触	jiēchù	v.	connect
11	之后	zhīhòu	n.	after
12	正常	zhèngcháng	adj.	normal
13	测量	cèliáng	v.	measure
14	电压	diànyā	n.	voltage
15	插座	chāzuò	n.	socket
16	数值	shùzhí	n.	reading

65

词语练习 Word Exercises

1. 认读词语。Recognize and read the words.

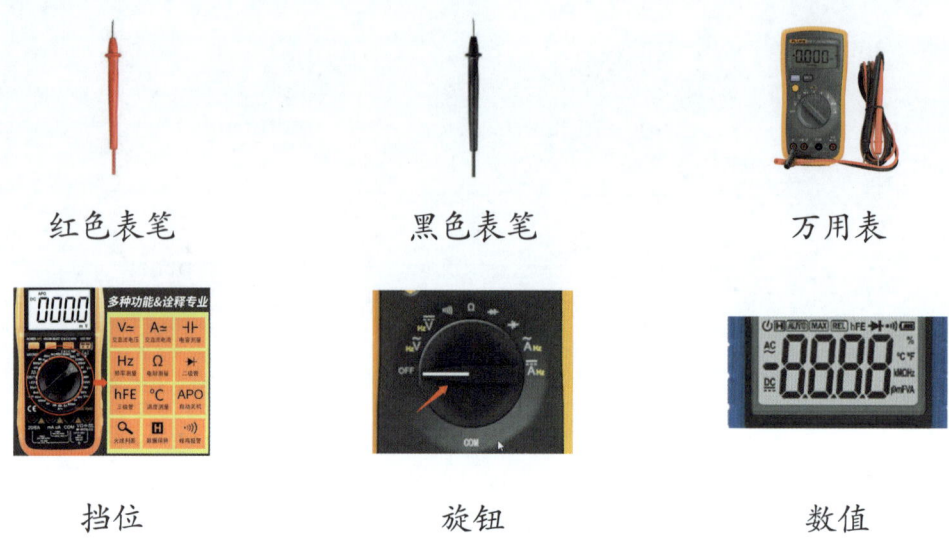

| 红色表笔 | 黑色表笔 | 万用表 |
| 挡位 | 旋钮 | 数值 |

2. 朗读词语搭配。Read aloud the word collocations.

❶ 选择	选择电压挡	
❷ 接触	接触表笔	
❸ 旋钮	转动旋钮	
❹ 测量	测量电压	

第 8 课 | 使用万用表

 学习课文 Text 🎧 08-02

使用 万用表
Shǐyòng wànyòngbiǎo

1. 把红色表笔和黑色表笔插入万用表；
Bǎ hóngsè biǎobǐ hé hēisè biǎobǐ chārù wànyòngbiǎo;

2. 转动旋钮，选择蜂鸣挡位；
Zhuàndòng xuánniǔ, xuǎnzé fēngmíng dǎngwèi;

3. 接触表笔之后有声音，说明万用表是正常的；
Jiēchù biǎobǐ zhīhòu yǒu shēngyīn, shuōmíng wànyòngbiǎo shì zhèngcháng de;

4. 转动旋钮，选择电压挡位后，再测量电压；
Zhuàndòng xuánniǔ, xuǎnzé diànyā dǎngwèi hòu, zài cèliáng diànyā;

5. 表笔插入插座，万用表有数值；
Biǎobǐ chārù chāzuò, wànyòngbiǎo yǒu shùzhí;

6. 测量后，选择 OFF 挡位，关闭万用表。
Cèliáng hòu, xuǎnzé OFF dǎngwèi, guānbì wànyòngbiǎo.

Use the Multimeter

1. Insert the red probe and black probe into the multimeter;

2. Rotate the knob to select the buzz level;

3. After connecting the probes, the multimeter is normal if it beeps;

4. Rotate the knob and select the level for voltage measuring;

5. Insert the probes into the socket and note down the readings;

6. After measuring, select OFF to switch off the multimeter.

课文练习 Text Exercises

1. 选择正确的顺序。Choose the right order.

①把表笔插入万用表　　　　②转动旋钮，选择蜂鸣挡位

③转动旋钮，选择电压挡位　　④表笔插入插座，测量电压

⑤接触表笔，检查万用表　　　⑥关闭万用表

A. ③①④②⑤⑥　　　　B. ②①④③⑥⑤　　　　C. ①②⑤③④⑥

正确的顺序为（　　）。

The right order is (　　).

2. 选词填空。Choose the words to fill in the blanks.

❶ 表笔要（　　）万用表。　　　　A. 转动　　B. 插入

❷ 用蜂鸣（　　）检查万用表。　　A. 挡位　　B. 旋钮

❸ 选择挡位后，万用表有（　　）。　A. 数值　　B. 电压

❹ 测量电压后，（　　）要关闭。　　A. 万用表　B. 表笔

学习语法 Grammar

 语法点1 Grammar Point 1

……后/之后，……

As an adverbial in sentences, "……后/之后，……" means "one thing happens after another". For example,

例句	英文翻译
Biǎobǐ chārù wànyòngbiǎo hòu, zài shǐyòng wànyòngbiǎo. 表笔插入万用表后，再使用万用表。	Insert the probes before you use the multimeter.
Shǐyòng wànyòngbiǎo zhīhòu, yào guānbì wànyòngbiǎo. 使用万用表之后，要关闭万用表。	Switch off the multimeter after using it.
Jiēchù biǎobǐ zhīhòu, yǒu shēngyīn, shuōmíng wànyòngbiǎo shì zhèngcháng de. 接触表笔之后，有声音，说明万用表是正常的。	After connecting the probes, the multimeter is normal if it beeps.

选词填空。Choose the words to fill in the blanks.

1. 盘车救援（　　），要断开电源。　　A. 前　　B. 之后
2. 表笔插入万用表（　　），再接触表笔。　　A. 前　　B. 之后
3. 维保电梯（　　），要准备工具。　　A. 前　　B. 之后
4. 测量电压（　　），万用表要关闭。　　A. 前　　B. 之后

 语法点 2 **Grammar Point 2**

副词"再"　The Adverb "再"

"再" indicates that an action takes place after the completion of another. A sentence usually goes like "a phrasal verb (+ 后),再 + another phrasal verb". For example,

例句	英文翻译
Biǎobǐ chārù wànyòngbiǎo zài zhuàndòng xuánniǔ. 表笔插入万用表再转动旋钮。	Insert the probes into the multimeter, and then rotate the knob.
Xuǎnzé fēngmíng dǎngwèi zài jiēchù biǎobǐ. 选择蜂鸣挡位再接触表笔。	Select the buzz level, and then connect the probes.
Xuǎnzé diànyā dǎngwèi zài cèliáng diànyā. 选择电压挡位再测量电压。	Select the voltage level, and then measure the voltage.

改写句子。Rewrite the sentences.

1. 工作前，要戴上安全帽。
   _____再_____。

2. 更换润滑油前，要断开电源。
   _____再_____。

3. 到机房前，先把护栏放好。
   _____，再_____。

4. 断开电源前，先准备锁和标牌。
   _____，再_____。

 汉字书写 Writing Chinese Characters

文化拓展 Culture Insight

饺子 Chinese Dumplings

Chinese dumplings, or *jiaozi*, are a traditional food with distinctive Chinese characteristics. They look like shoe-shaped gold ingots and symbolize wealth and family reunion. With the arrival of the Spring Festival, almost every family is busy preparing dumplings. The skin of dumplings is as thin as a cicada's wing, and they are filled with delicious stuffing—pork, leek, and shrimp… After taking a bite, the delicious soup of the dumplings splashes everywhere, which makes people feel that it is the real human delicacy. Dumplings are not only delicious food, but also bear Chinese people's wish for a wonderful life.

小结 Summary

朗读下列词语。Read aloud the following words.

选择	正常	表笔	万用表
测量	接触	插座	使用
数值	之后		

语法 Grammar

朗读下列句子。Read aloud the following sentences.

1. 接触表笔之后，有声音，说明万用表是正常的。
2. 使用万用表后，要关闭万用表。
3. 选择电压挡位后，再测量电压。
4. 测量电压后，再选择 OFF 挡位，关闭万用表。

课文理解 Text Comprehension

复述课文内容。Retell the text.

1. 把红色……和黑色……插入万用表。
2. 转动……，选择……挡位。
3. ……表笔之后，有……，说明万用表……的。
4. 转动……，选择电压……后，再……电压。
5. ……插入插座，万用表……。
6. 测量后，选择 OFF 挡位，……万用表。

第 9 课 Lesson 9

Cèshì jǐnjí diàndòng yùnxíng
测试紧急电动运行
Test the Emergency Power Operation (EPO)

复习 Revision

根据上一课课文选图填空。Choose the pictures to fill in the blanks based on the previous text.

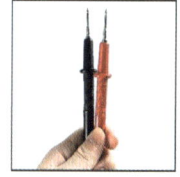

A.

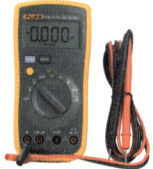

B.

C.

D.

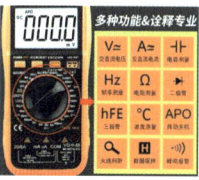

E.

1 转动_____以后，再使用_____。

2 选择_____后，再使用_____测量_____的电压。

73

 ## 热身 Warm-up

看图连线。Look at the pictures and match them with the words.

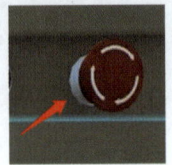    

xiàxíng	shàngxíng ànniǔ	xiàxíng ànniǔ	jítíng kāiguān	shàngxíng
下行	上行 按钮	下行 按钮	急停 开关	上行
going down	the up button	the down button	the stop button	going up

 ## 学习生词 Words and Expressions  09-01

1	测试	cèshì	v./n.	test
2	紧急电动运行	jǐnjí diàndòng yùnxíng	phr.	emergency power operation (EPO)
3	务必	wùbì	adv.	must
4	确认	quèrèn	v.	make sure
5	没有	méiyǒu	v.	there is /are not, not have
6	进入	jìnrù	v.	enter
7	紧急电动开关	jǐnjí diàndòng kāiguān	phr.	EPO switch

第 9 课 | 测试紧急电动运行

8	状态	zhuàngtài	*n.*	mode, state
9	按	àn	*v.*	press
10	上行	shàngxíng	*v.*	go up
11	按钮	ànniǔ	*n.*	button
12	能	néng	*opt.*	can
13	下行	xiàxíng	*v.*	go down
14	急停开关	jítíng kāiguān	*phr.*	the stop button

 词语练习 **Word Exercises**

1. 认读词语。**Recognize and read the words.**

　急停开关　　　　　　　上行　　　　　　　紧急电动开关

　上行按钮　　　　　　　下行　　　　　　　下行按钮

2. 朗读词语搭配。Read aloud the word collocations.

❶ 开关	紧急电动开关	
	急停开关	
❷ 按钮	上行按钮	
	下行按钮	
❸ 电梯	电梯上行	
	电梯下行	
❹ 按	按开关	
	按按钮	

第 9 课 | 测试紧急电动运行

 **学习课文 Text** 🎧 09-02

测试 紧急电动 运行
Cèshì jǐnjí diàndòng yùnxíng

Wùbì quèrèn jiàoxiāng lǐmiàn méiyǒu chéngkè. Diàntīgōng jìnrù jīfáng, xuánzhuǎn jǐnjí diàndòng kāiguān, diàntī dào jǐnjí diàndòng yùnxíng zhuàngtài. Àn shàngxíng ànniǔ, diàntī néng shàngxíng; àn xiàxíng ànniǔ, diàntī néng xiàxíng. Ànxia jítíng kāiguān, diàntī bù néng yùnxíng.

务必 确认 轿厢 里面 没有 乘客。电梯工 进入 机房，旋转 紧急 电动 开关，电梯 到 紧急 电动 运行 状态。按 上行 按钮，电梯 能 上行；按 下行 按钮，电梯 能 下行。按下 急停开关，电梯 不能 运行。

Test the Emergency Power Operation (EPO)

Make sure there are no passengers in the elevator car. The elevator worker enters the machine room and rotates the switch to keep the elevator in the "Emergency Power Operation (EPO)" mode. The elevator goes up/down if one presses the corresponding switch. The elevator doesn't go if one presses the stop button.

课文练习 Text Exercises

1. 判断对错。Tell whether the following statements are true (T) or false (F).

   ① 测试紧急电动运行时，轿厢里面不能有乘客。　　　　（　　）
   ② 电梯工要测试上行按钮和下行按钮。　　　　　　　　（　　）
   ③ 按下急停开关后，电梯能上行。　　　　　　　　　　（　　）
   ④ 测试时，按上行按钮和下行按钮，电梯能运行。　　　（　　）

2. 选词填空。Choose the words to fill in the blanks.

   ① （　　）没有乘客后，再进行测试。　　A. 确认　　B. 务必
   ② 测试时，电梯要（　　）紧急电动运行状态。
   　　　　　　　　　　　　　　　　　　　A. 进入　　B. 打开
   ③ 按上行按钮，电梯能（　　）。　　　　A. 上行　　B. 下行
   ④ 测试上行按钮后，再测试（　　）。　　A. 下行按钮　B. 急停开关

学习语法 Grammar

语法点1 Grammar Point 1

副词"务必" The Adverb "务必"

"务必" is usually used before a verb, meaning that something must be done. For example,

例句	英文翻译
Wéibǎo diàntī shí, wùbì yào dài ānquánmào. 维保电梯时，务必要戴安全帽。	One must wear a safety helmet when maintaining the elevator.

（续表）

例句	英文翻译
Pánchē jiùyuán qián, wùbì yào duànkāi diànyuán. 盘车 救援 前，务必要 断开 电源。	The power supply must be disconnected before the handwheel rescue.
Diàntī kùnrén shí, wùbì yào jìnxíng jiùyuán. 电梯 困人 时，务必要 进行 救援。	Passengers must be rescued when they get trapped in an elevator.

改写句子。**Rewrite the sentences.**

1. 维保电梯时，要戴上安全帽。
   _____务必_____。

2. 更换润滑油前，要断开电源。
   _____务必_____。

3. 盘车救援前，先断开电源。
   _____务必_____。

4. 测量电压前，要检查万用表。
   _____务必_____。

语法点 2 Grammar Point 2

能愿动词"能" The Optative Verb "能"

"能" indicates that it is possible or allowed to do something. It is often used in questions or negative sentences. For example,

例句	英文翻译
Yòng sānjiǎo yàoshi néng dǎkāi céngmén. 用 三角 钥匙 能 打开 层门。	One can use the triangular key to open the landing door.
Àn shàngxíng ànniǔ, diàntī bù néng xiàxíng. 按 上行 按钮，电梯不能 下行。	The elevator can't go down if one presses the up button.

例句	英文翻译
Pánchē jiùyuán néng yídòng jiàoxiāng. 盘车 救援 能 移动 轿厢。	One can move the elevator car in the handwheel rescue.

(续表)

选词填空。Choose the words to fill in the blanks.

1. 按下上行按钮，电梯（　　）上行。　　A. 要　　B. 能
2. 维保电梯（　　）注意安全。　　　　　A. 要　　B. 能
3. 护栏（　　）防止乘客进入轿厢。　　　A. 要　　B. 能
4. 电梯工（　　）检查曳引机。　　　　　A. 要　　B. 能

 汉字书写 Writing Chinese Characters

bái 白 白 白 白 白
白 白 白 白 白

zì 自 自 自 自 自
自 自 自 自 自

bǎi 百 百 百 百 百 百
百 百 百 百 百

pāi 拍 拍 拍 拍 拍 拍 拍 拍
拍 拍 拍 拍 拍

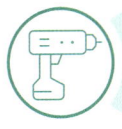

职业拓展 Career Insight

液压式升降机 Hydraulic Elevator

In 1845, William Thompson made the world's first hydraulic elevator, which is a mechanical device that uses the compression of fluid (water at that time) to generate movement. Its main components include the hydraulic cylinder, piston, piston rod, oil pump, oil tank and valve. The pump draws oil from the oil tank and channels it through the valve that regulates its flow. Once pressurized, the oil will be sent to the hydraulic cylinder to make the piston and the connected rod move vertically in a reciprocating manner. This movement in turn drives the lifting platform or hanging basket to rise. Hydraulic elevators are widely used in industries such as industrial manufacturing, construction and warehousing because of their simple structure, stable operation, high bearing capacity and good maintainability.

 小结 Summary

词语 Words

朗读下列词语。Read aloud the following words.

测试	状态	按	运行
进入	紧急电动开关	急停开关	下行按钮
上行	能		

语法 Grammar

朗读下列句子。Read aloud the following sentences.

1. 测试紧急电动运行前，务必确认轿厢里面没有乘客。
2. 测试紧急电动运行时，务必测试上行按钮和下行按钮。
3. 按下上行按钮，电梯能上行。
4. 按下急停开关，电梯不能运行。

课文理解 Text Comprehension

复述课文内容。Retell the text.

1. 测试……，务必确认……里面没有……。
2. 电梯工……机房，旋转……，电梯到紧急电动……。
3. 按……，电梯能上行；按下行按钮，电梯………。
4. 按下………，电梯……运行。

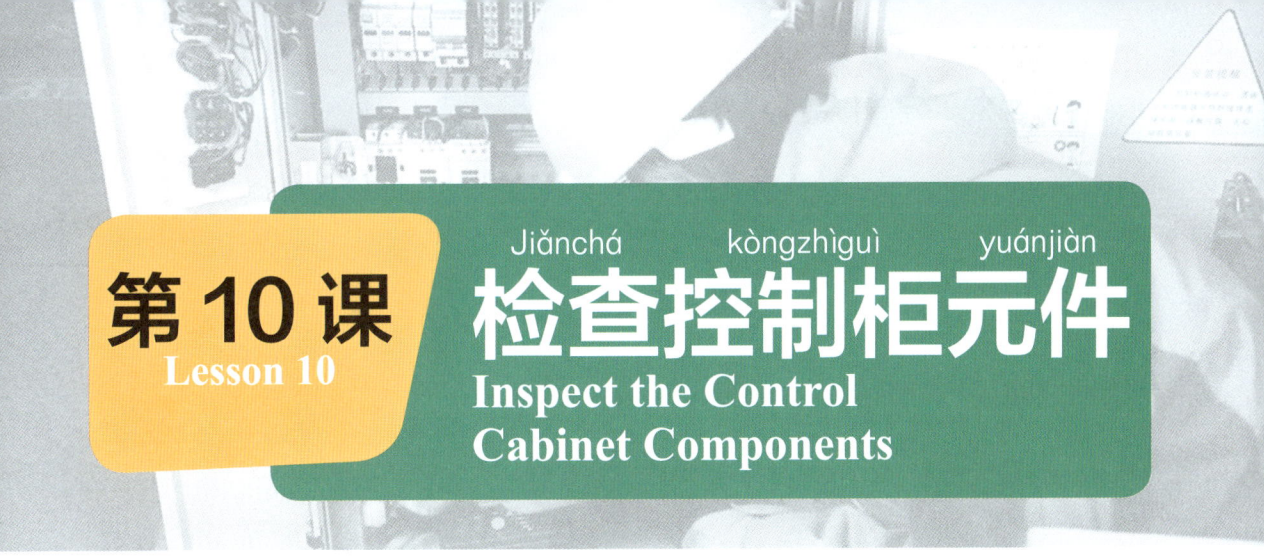

第10课 Lesson 10

Jiǎnchá kòngzhìguì yuánjiàn
检查控制柜元件
Inspect the Control Cabinet Components

 复习 Revision

根据上一课课文选图填空。Choose the pictures to fill in the blanks based on the previous text.

A.   B.   C.

1. 电梯工进入_____，旋转_____，再按_____。

 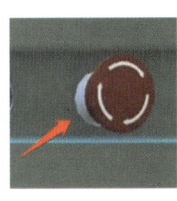

A.   B.   C.

2. 测试紧急电动运行，先测试_____和_____，再按_____。

 ## 热身 Warm-up

看图读词语。Look at the pictures and read the words.

jiēchùqì
接触器
contactor

jìdiànqì
继电器
relay

jiēxiàn duānzi
接线端子
wiring terminal

biànyāqì
变压器
transformer

kāiguān diànyuán
开关 电源
switch power supply

chājiàn
插件
plug-in

 ## 学习生词 Words and Expressions 10-01

1	元件	yuánjiàn	n.	component
2	接触器	jiēchùqì	n.	contactor
3	继电器	jìdiànqì	n.	relay
4	确保	quèbǎo	v.	make sure
5	各	gè	pron.	every
6	接线端子	jiēxiàn duānzi	phr.	wiring terminal

7	插件	chājiàn	n.	plug-in
8	固定	gùdìng	v.	secure
9	情况	qíngkuàng	n.	situation
10	清理	qīnglǐ	v.	clean, remove dust from
11	变压器	biànyāqì	n.	transformer
12	开关电源	kāiguān diànyuán	phr.	switch power supply
13	等	děng	part.	etc.
14	灰尘	huīchén	n.	dust
15	恢复	huīfù	v.	restore

词语练习 Word Exercises

1. 认读词语。Recognize and read the words.

接触器　　　　　　继电器　　　　　　接线端子

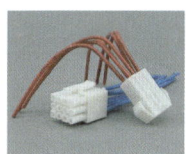  

插件　　　　　　变压器　　　　　　开关电源

2. 朗读词语搭配。Read aloud the word collocations.

❶ 检查	检查接触器	
	检查接线端子	
❷ 清理	清理灰尘	
❸ 恢复	恢复电源	

学习课文 Text  10-02

检查 控制柜 元件
Jiǎnchá kòngzhìguì yuánjiàn

Dǎkāi kòngzhìguì, diàntī zhuǎnhuàn dào jiǎnxiū zhuàngtài, jiǎn-
打开 控制柜，电梯 转换 到 检修 状态，检

chá jiēchùqì、jìdiànqì, quèbǎo zhèngcháng。Duànkāi diànyuán,
查 接触器、继电器，确保 正常。断开 电源，

jiǎnchá gè jiēxiàn duānzi hé chājiàn de gùdìng qíngkuàng, qīnglǐ
检查 各接线 端子 和 插件 的 固定 情况，清理

第 10 课 | 检查控制柜元件

变压器、开关电源等元件上的灰尘。恢复电源，测量元件的电压，确保正常。

Inspect the Control Cabinet Components

Open the control cabinet and switch the elevator into the "Inspection" mode. Examine the contactors and relays to ensure their normal operation. Disconnect the power supply to check if every wiring terminal and plug-in is secured, and remove dust from the components such as transformers, switch power supplies, etc. Restore the power, and measure the voltage of the components to ensure their normal operation.

课文练习 Text Exercises

1. 判断对错。Tell whether the following statements are true (T) or false (F).

    ① 检查控制柜时，电梯是检修状态。　　　　　　　　　（　　）
    ② 检查插件前，要恢复电源。　　　　　　　　　　　　（　　）
    ③ 变压器和开关电源在控制柜外面。　　　　　　　　　（　　）
    ④ 检查控制柜时，要测量各元件的电压。　　　　　　　（　　）

2. 选词填空。Choose the words to fill in the blanks.

    ① 断开电源后，再检查接线端子的（　　）情况。　　A. 固定　　B. 安全
    ② 检查控制柜时，要清理（　　）上的灰尘。　　　　A. 元件　　B. 电源
    ③ 清理灰尘后，需要（　　）电梯的电源。　　　　　A. 恢复　　B. 断开
    ④ 控制柜里面各元件要（　　）正常。　　　　　　　A. 确保　　B. 确认

学习语法 Grammar

 语法点 1　Grammar Point 1

指示代词"各"　The Demonstrative Pronoun "各"

"各" is used before a noun and refers to each individual in a large number of people or things. For example,

例句	英文翻译
Qīnglǐ kòngzhìguì lǐmiàn gè yuánjiàn shang de huīchén. 清理 控制柜 里面 各 元件 上 的 灰尘。	Remove dust from each component in the control cabinet.
Duànkāi diànyuán hòu, jiǎnchá gè chājiàn de gùdìng qíngkuàng. 断开 电源 后，检查 各 插件 的 固定 情况。	After disconnecting the power, check if each plug-in is secured.
Jīfáng lǐmiàn de gè yuánjiàn dōu yào jiǎnchá. 机房 里面 的 各 元件 都 要 检查。	All the components in the machine room needs inspection.

连词成句。Rearrange the words into sentences.

1 ①检查　②都　③各　④元件　⑤要

　→ _____

2 ①检查　②位置　③都　④要　⑤各

　→ _____

3 ①都　②要　③各　④准备　⑤工具

　→ _____

4 ①各　②检查　③元件　④控制柜　⑤里面　⑥的　⑦固定　⑧情况

　→ _____

第 10 课 | 检查控制柜元件

 语法点 2 Grammar Point 2

助词"等" The Auxiliary Word "等"

"等" indicates that there are more items in a series or list, without explicitly mentioning all of them. For example,

例句	英文翻译
Qīnglǐ kāiguān diànyuán、biànyāqì děng yuánjiàn shang de huīchén. 清理开关 电源、变压器 等 元件 上 的 灰尘。	Remove dust from the components, such as switch power supplies, transformers, etc.
Jīfáng、céngmén děng wèizhì dōu yào jiǎnchá. 机房、层门 等 位置 都 要 检查。	It is necessary to inspect the machine room, the landing door, etc.
Jīfáng lǐmiàn yǒu biāopái、suǒ děng gōngjù. 机房 里面 有 标牌、锁 等 工具。	Tools like labels, locks, etc. are in the machine room.

选词填空。Choose the words to fill in the blanks.

1. 控制柜里面有接触器、继电器（　　）元件。　　A. 各　　B. 等
2. 电梯工要清理（　　）元件上的灰尘。　　A. 各　　B. 等
3. 电梯机房、轿厢（　　）位置都有插件。　　A. 各　　B. 等
4. 断开电源、放护栏（　　）工作都是为了安全。　　A. 各　　B. 等

 **汉字书写** Writing Chinese Characters

huǒ
火 火 火 火
火 火 火 火 火

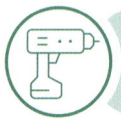 **文化拓展 Culture Insight**

火药 Gunpowder

Gunpowder originated in ancient China and is one of China's Four Great Inventions. The application of gunpowder in military affairs changed the way wars were fought. After gunpowder was introduced to the West, it made great contributions to the development of weapons in the West and promoted the development of world history. The invention of gunpowder reflects the wisdom and innovation of ancient Chinese in chemistry and metallurgy, and has a positive impact on the scientific research and technological development of later generations.

第 10 课 | 检查控制柜元件

小结 Summary

词语 Words

朗读下列词语。Read aloud the following words.

清理	恢复	各	灰尘
等	接触器	继电器	开关电源
接线端子	变压器		

语法 Grammar

朗读下列句子。Read aloud the following sentences.

1. 清理控制柜里各元件上的灰尘。
2. 断开电源后，检查各接线端子和插件的固定情况。
3. 清理变压器、开关电源等元件上的灰尘。
4. 控制柜里有接触器、继电器等元件。

课文理解 Text Comprehension

复述课文内容。Retell the text.

1. 打开……，电梯转换到……，检查……、……，确保正常。
2. 断开电源，检查……接线端子和……。
3. 清理……、……等……的灰尘。
4. ……电源，测量……，……正常。

第 11 课 Lesson 11

Shìfàng zhìdòngqì jīxiènéng
释放制动器机械能
Release the Mechanical Energy of the Brake

 **复习 Revision**

根据上一课课文选图填空。Choose the pictures to fill in the blanks based on the previous text.

　　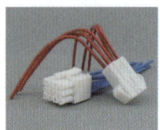　　　　

　A.　　　　　　　B.　　　　　　　C.　　　　　　　D.

检查控制柜里_____和_____的固定情况，清理_____、_____等元件上的灰尘。

 **热身 Warm-up**

看图连线。Look at the pictures and match them with the words.

tíngzhǐ　　　céngzhàn　　　huǎnchōngqì　　　duìzhòng
停止　　　　层站　　　　　缓冲器　　　　　对重
stop　　　　landing　　　　buffer　　　　　counterweight

第 11 课 ｜ 释放制动器机械能

 学习生词 Words and Expressions 🎧 11-01

1	释放	shìfàng	v.	release
2	机械能	jīxiènéng	n.	mechanical energy
3	顶层	dǐngcéng	n.	top floor
4	层站	céngzhàn	n.	landing
5	并	bìng	conj.	and
6	对重	duìzhòng	n.	counterweight
7	开始	kāishǐ	v.	start, begin
8	最后	zuìhòu	n.	(in the) end
9	压紧	yājǐn	phr.	be pressed (tight)
10	缓冲器	huǎnchōngqì	n.	buffer
11	停止	tíngzhǐ	v.	stop

词语练习 Word Exercises

1. 认读词语。Recognize and read the words.

缓冲器

对重

停止　　　　　　　顶层　　　　　　　层站

2. 朗读词语搭配。Read aloud the word collocations.

❶ 制动器	松开制动器	
❷ 层站	层站按钮	
❸ 压紧	压紧缓冲器	
❹ 顶层	电梯的顶层	

第 11 课 | 释放制动器机械能

 学习课文 Text 🎧 11-02

释放 制动器 机械能
Shìfàng zhìdòngqì jīxiènéng

电梯工 A 在顶层按下层站按钮。电梯到顶层后，确认轿厢里面没有乘客。电梯工 B 在机房断开电源并锁上电源盒，松开制动器后，对重开始下行。最后压紧缓冲器，对重停止下行，电梯没有移动。

Release the Mechanical Energy of the Brake

Elevator worker A presses the landing button on the top floor. Make sure that there are no passengers in the elevator car when the elevator reaches the top. In the machine room, elevator worker B disconnects the power supply and locks the power box. After releasing the brake, the counterweight starts to go down until the buffer is pressed tight. The counterweight stops, and the elevator doesn't move.

课文练习 Text Exercises

1. 判断对错。Tell whether the following statements are true (T) or false (F).

   ① 断开电源前,先确认轿厢里面没有乘客。　　　　　　　　(　　)
   ② 松开制动器前,要先断开电源。　　　　　　　　　　　　(　　)
   ③ 松开制动器的操作要在机房进行。　　　　　　　　　　　(　　)
   ④ 对重压紧缓冲器后,电梯没有移动。　　　　　　　　　　(　　)

2. 选词填空。Choose the words to fill in the blanks.

   ① 电梯到顶层后,(　　)里没有乘客。
      A. 缓冲器　　　B. 轿厢　　　C. 对重　　　D. 电源盒
   ② 松开制动器后,(　　)下行。
      A. 缓冲器　　　B. 轿厢　　　C. 对重　　　D. 电源盒
   ③ 对重压紧(　　)后,电梯停止移动。
      A. 缓冲器　　　B. 轿厢　　　C. 对重　　　D. 电源盒
   ④ 断开电源后要锁上(　　)。
      A. 缓冲器　　　B. 轿厢　　　C. 对重　　　D. 电源盒

学习语法 Grammar

语法点 1 Grammar Point 1

介词"在"　The Preposition "在"

"在" indicates a location in which some action takes place. It is usually used in the sentence structure "在 + phrasal noun + phrasal verb". Sometimes, the structure "phrasal verb + 在 + phrasal noun" is used to indicate the location where an action ends. For example,

第 11 课 | 释放制动器机械能

例句	英文翻译
Diàntīgōng zài dǐngcéng ànxia céngzhàn ànniǔ. 电梯工在 顶层 按下 层站 按钮。	The elevator worker presses the landing button on the top floor.
Wǒ zài jīfáng jiǎnchá kòngzhìguì. 我在机房 检查 控制柜。	I am inspecting the control cabinet in the machine room.
Bǎ ānquánmào fàng zài jiàoxiāng li. 把安全帽 放 在轿厢里。	Put the safety helmet in the elevator car.

连词成句。Rearrange the words into sentences.

1. ①在　②机房　③释放　④机械能　⑤我
   → _____
2. ①轿厢　②放　③我　④护栏　⑤里面　⑥在
   → _____
3. ①盘车　②救援　③机房　④在　⑤电梯工　⑥进行
   → _____
4. ①我　②测量　③控制柜　④里面　⑤在　⑥电压
   → _____

语法点 2 Grammar Point 2

连词"并" The Conjunction "并"

"并" can be used to connect verbs, adjectives, etc., indicating that these actions happen (or these attributes exist) at the same time. For example,

例句	英文翻译
Jìnrù jīfáng, duànkāi diànyuán bìng suǒshang diànyuánhé. 进入 机房, 断开 电源 并 锁上 电源盒。	Enter the machine room, disconnect the power supply and lock the power box.

(续表)

例句	英文翻译
Guānbì diànyuánhé bìng guàshang biāopái. 关闭 电源盒 并 挂上 标牌。	Turn off the power box and put up a sign.
Dàishang ānquánmào bìng kāishǐ gōngzuò. 戴上 安全帽 并开始 工作。	Wear a safety helmet and start to work.

选词填空。Choose the words to fill in the blanks.

1. 我（　　）他都是电梯工。
   A. 和　　　　　　B. 并　　　　　　C. 或者

2. 进入机房后，断开（　　）锁上电源。
   A. 和　　　　　　B. 并　　　　　　C. 或者

3. 电梯有故障（　　）困人时，要进行盘车救援。
   A. 和　　　　　　B. 并　　　　　　C. 或者

4. 断开控制柜电源，（　　）检查各元件。
   A. 和　　　　　　B. 并　　　　　　C. 或者

汉字书写 Writing Chinese Characters

cái
才　才　才　才
才　才　才　才

cùn
寸　寸　寸
寸　寸　寸　寸

duì
对　对　对　对　对
对　对　对　对　对

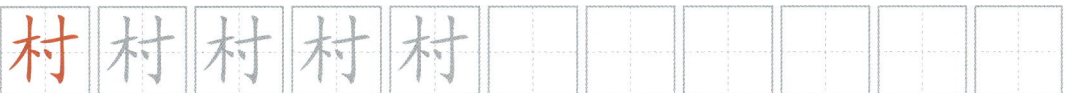

cūn 村 村 村 村 村 村 村
村 村 村 村 村

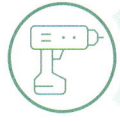
文化拓展 Culture Insight

自动扶梯 Escalator

Escalator is a fixed electrical device that diagonally transports passengers between floors in a building. It evolved from a human-/animal-powered lifting device in old days. The first escalator was described in a US patent issued to Nathan Ames, yet it was not until 1900 that the device made its debut at the Paris Expo. After a decade, Otis Elevator Company bought and updated the patent to make modern escalators. Escalators have a wide range of applications, such as public transportation facilities, shopping malls, airports, and exhibition centers, etc. They provide a convenient, comfortable, and safe mode of vertical mobility.

小结 Summary

词语 Words

朗读下列词语。Read aloud the following words.

层站　　　最后　　　并　　　顶层

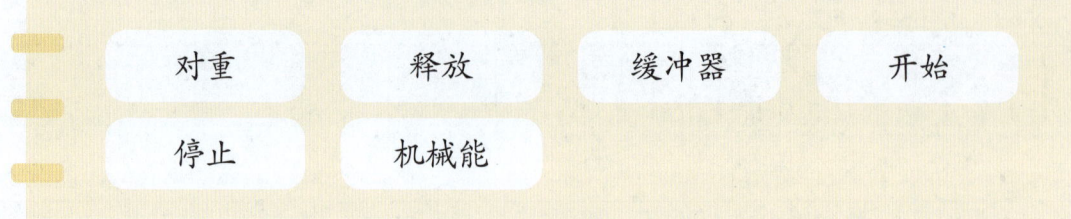

语法 Grammar

朗读下列句子。Read aloud the following sentences.

1. 我在机房检查控制柜。
2. 电梯工在顶层按下层站按钮。
3. 进入机房，断开电源并锁上电源盒。
4. 关闭电源盒并挂上标牌。

课文理解 Text Comprehension

复述课文内容。Retell the text.

1. 电梯工 A 在顶层……。
2. 电梯……后，确认……。
3. 电梯工 B 在机房断开……并锁上……，松开……，……开始下行。
4. 最后……，……停止下行，电梯……。

第 12 课
Lesson 12

Jiǎnchá zhìdòngqì
检查制动器
Inspect the Brake

 **复习 Revision**

根据上一课课文选图填空。Choose the pictures to fill in the blanks based on the previous text.

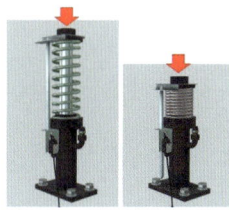

A.　　　　　　　　　　B.　　　　　　　　　　C.

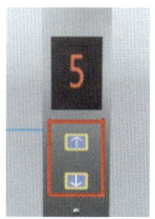

D.　　　　　　　　　　　　　　E.

在_____按下_____，再_____，_____，对重下行，最后_____，对重停止下行，电梯没有移动。

 ## 热身 Warm-up

看图连线。Look at the pictures and match them with the words.

  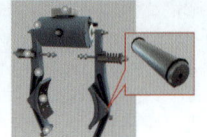 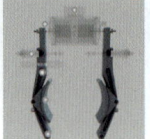 

zhìdòngbì	xiāozhóu	zhùsāi dǐnggǎn	tánhuáng	duànliè
制动臂	销轴	柱塞顶杆	弹簧	断裂
brake arm	pin shaft	plunger push rod	spring	break

 ## 学习生词 Words and Expressions 🎧 12-01

1	销轴	xiāozhóu	n.	pin shaft
2	是否	shìfǒu	adv.	whether / if (or not)
3	锈迹	xiùjì	n.	rust
4	弹簧	tánhuáng	n.	spring
5	断裂	duànliè	v.	break
6	把	bǎ	m.	a measure word quantifying objects that have a handle or can be held
7	直尺	zhíchǐ	n.	ruler
8	长度	chángdù	n.	length

9	标尺	biāochǐ	n.	scale
10	相同	xiāngtóng	adj.	same
11	柱塞顶杆	zhùsāi dǐnggǎn	phr.	plunger push rod
12	制动臂	zhìdòngbì	n.	brake arm
13	之间	zhījiān	n.	between
14	间隙	jiànxì	n.	clearance
15	范围	fànwéi	n.	range
16	内	nèi	n.	within

词语练习 Word Exercises

1. 认读词语。Recognize and read the words.

弹簧

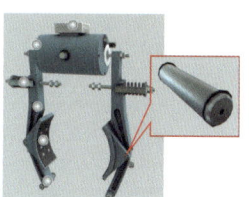
锈迹

销轴

直尺

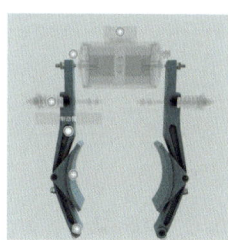
制动臂

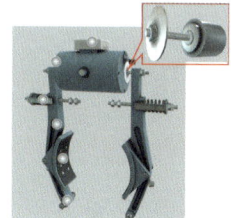
柱塞

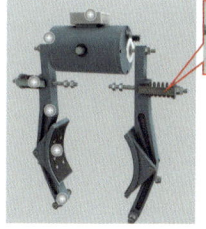
标尺

2. 朗读词语搭配。Read aloud the word collocations.

❶ 柱塞	柱塞顶杆	
❷ 销轴	销轴锈迹	
❸ 弹簧	弹簧长度	
	弹簧断裂	
❹ 间隙	测量间隙	

学习课文 Text 🎧 12-02

Jiǎnchá zhìdòngqì
检查 制动器

Duànkāi diànyuán, guānchá zhìdòngqì, kàn xiāozhóu shìfǒu yǒu
断开 电源，观察 制动器，看 销轴 是否 有
xiùjì, zài kàn tánhuáng shìfǒu duànliè. Yòng yì bǎ zhíchǐ cèliáng
锈迹，再看 弹簧 是否 断裂。用 一把 直尺 测量

第 12 课 | 检查制动器

tánhuáng chángdù, kàn shùzhí hé biāochǐ shang de shìfǒu xiāngtóng. Zài
弹簧 长度，看 数值 和 标尺 上 的 是否 相同。在
zhùsāi dǐnggǎn hé zhìdòngbì zhījiān cèliáng jiànxì, quèbǎo jiànxì
柱塞顶杆 和 制动臂 之间 测量 间隙，确保 间隙
zài zhèngcháng fànwéi nèi.
在 正常 范围 内。

Inspect the Brake

Disconnect the power supply and observe the brake to check if there is rust on the pin shaft and whether the spring is broken. Measure the length of the spring with a ruler to see if it is the same as the one on the scale. Then, measure the clearance between the plunger push rod and the brake arm to ensure the reading is within the normal range.

课文练习 Text Exercises

1. 判断对错。Tell whether the following statements are true (T) or false (F).

   1. 检查制动器要先断开电源。　　　　　　　　　　　　（　　）
   2. 要检查制动器弹簧是否断裂。　　　　　　　　　　　（　　）
   3. 弹簧的长度要和标尺相同。　　　　　　　　　　　　（　　）
   4. 检查制动器要用直尺。　　　　　　　　　　　　　　（　　）

2. 选词填空。Choose the words to fill in the blanks.

   1. 制动器的销轴不能有（　　）。　　　A. 断裂　　　B. 锈迹
   2. 柱塞顶杆和制动臂之间的间隙要在正常（　　）内。

      A. 位置　　　B. 范围

3 制动器上的弹簧不能（　　）。　　A. 断裂　　B. 故障

4 弹簧的长度要和标尺上的数值（　　）。　　A. 相同　　B. 正常

 学习语法 Grammar

语法点 1　Grammar Point 1

副词"是否"　The Adverb "是否"

"是否" means " whether/if (or not)". It mostly indicates doubt or a choice between two possibilities in written Chinese. It is usually used in the sentence structure "Subject + 是否 + Predicate". For example,

例句	英文翻译
Wǒmen yào kàn xiāozhóu shìfǒu yǒu xiùjì. 我们 要 看 销轴 是否有锈迹。	We need to check if there is rust on the pin shaft.
Wǒmen yào guānchá tánhuáng shìfǒu duànliè. 我们 要 观察 弹簧 是否断裂。	We need to see if the spring is broken.
Wǒmen yào jiǎnchá wànnéngbiǎo shìfǒu néng zhèngcháng gōngzuò. 我们 要 检查 万能表 是否能 正常 工作。	We need to check if the multi-meter is in normal operation.

改写句子。Rewrite the sentences.

1 观察变压器上是不是有灰尘。

　　　　　　　　　是否　　　　　　　　。

2 检查万用表是不是正常。

　　　　　　　　　是否　　　　　　　　。

第12课 | 检查制动器

3 确认轿厢里面有没有乘客。

　　_____ 是否 _____ 。

4 检查插件有没有固定好。

　　_____ 是否 _____ 。

语法点 2 Grammar Point 2

量词"把"　The Measure Word "把"

"把" is a measure word for something with a handle. For example,

例句	英文翻译
Yòng yì bǎ zhíchǐ cèliáng tánhuáng de chángdù. 用一把直尺测量弹簧的长度。	Measure the length of the spring with a ruler.
Yòng yì bǎ yàoshi dǎkāi jīfáng de mén. 用一把钥匙打开机房的门。	Open the door of the machine room with a key.
Yòng yì bǎ sānjiǎo yàoshi dǎkāi céngmén. 用一把三角钥匙打开层门。	Open the landing door with a triangle key.

选词填空。Choose the words to fill in the blanks.

1 为了打开层门，要准备一（　　）三角钥匙。　　A. 个　　B. 把

2 层门外面有一（　　）直尺。　　　　　　　　A. 个　　B. 把

3 轿厢里面有三（　　）乘客。　　　　　　　　A. 个　　B. 把

4 检查控制柜要准备一（　　）万用表。　　　　A. 个　　B. 把

 汉字书写 Writing Chinese Characters

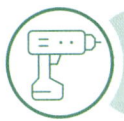 文化拓展 Culture Insight

熊猫 Giant Panda

Giant pandas are very adorable. They are fat and walk slowly with eye-catching black and white fur coats, as if they are reflecting on life. They have shiny black eyes and always look at their surroundings with insatiable curiosity. Although they look lazy, they have flexible limbs when eating bamboo. Giant pandas are not only China's national treasure, but are also a globally protected species. Their cuteness makes them deeply loved by people all over the world.

小结 Summary

词语 Words

朗读下列词语。Read aloud the following words.

制动臂	把	直尺	断裂
是否	弹簧	销轴	长度
间隙	相同		

语法 Grammar

朗读下列句子。Read aloud the following sentences.

1. 我们要看制动器销轴是否有锈迹。
2. 我们要观察弹簧是否断裂。
3. 用一把直尺测量弹簧的长度。
4. 用一把三角钥匙打开层门。

课文理解 Text Comprehension

复述课文内容。Retell the text.

1. 断开……，观察……，看销轴……，再看……。
2. 用一把直尺……，看数值和……相同。
3. 在……之间测量……，确保……在……内。

第 13 课 Lesson 13
Cèliáng zhìdòngqì jiànxì
测量制动器间隙
Measure the Clearances of the Brake

 复习 Revision

根据图片选择词语。Choose the words based on the pictures.

❶ 缓冲器（　　）
　 弹簧（　　）

❷ 柱塞（　　）
　 制动器（　　）

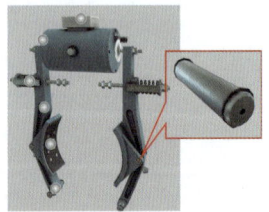

❸ 销轴（　　）
　 插件（　　）

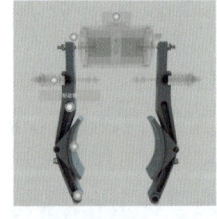

❹ 曳引机（　　）
　 制动臂（　　）

第 13 课 | 测量制动器间隙

热身 Warm-up

看图连线。Look at the pictures and match them with the words.

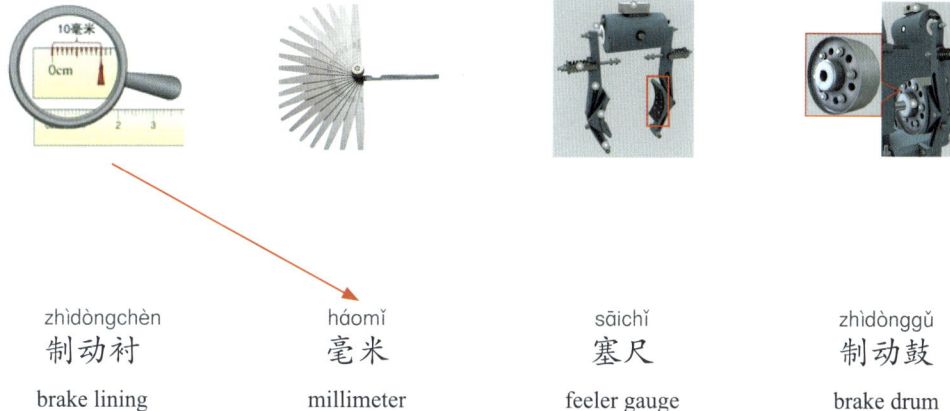

zhìdòngchèn	háomǐ	sāichǐ	zhìdònggǔ
制动衬	毫米	塞尺	制动鼓
brake lining	millimeter	feeler gauge	brake drum

学习生词 Words and Expressions 🎧 13-01

1	查看	chákàn	v.	check
2	制动衬	zhìdòngchèn	n.	brake lining
3	制动鼓	zhìdònggǔ	n.	brake drum
4	可以	kěyǐ	opt.	can
5	完全	wánquán	adv.	completely
6	贴合	tiēhé	v.	fit
7	塞尺	sāichǐ	n.	feeler gauge
8	大于	dàyú	v.	be greater/larger than
9	毫米	háomǐ	m.	millimeter (mm)

111

10	上端	shàngduān	n.	upper end
11	下端	xiàduān	n.	lower end
12	则	zé	conj.	then, hence
13	符合	fúhé	v.	accord with, be in line with
14	要求	yāoqiú	n.	requirement

词语练习 Word Exercises

1. 认读词语。Recognize and read the words.

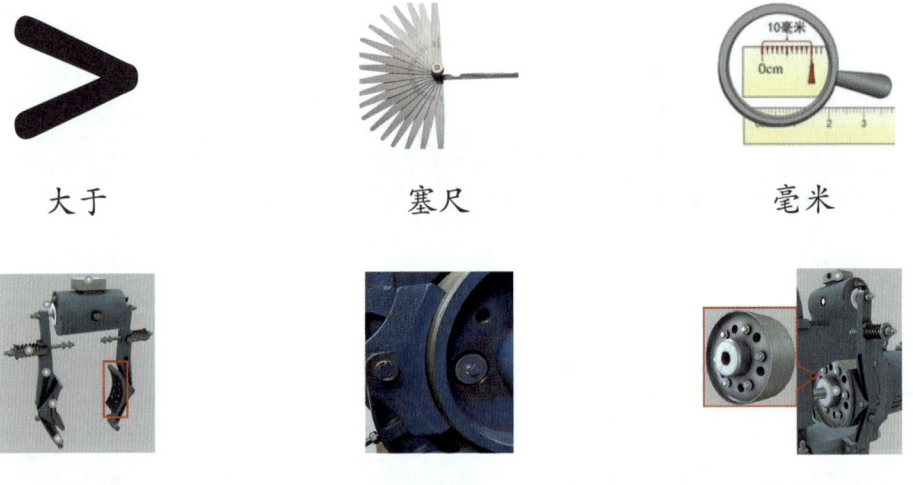

大于　　　　　塞尺　　　　　毫米

制动衬　　　　贴合　　　　　制动鼓

2. 朗读词语搭配。Read aloud the word collocations.

| ❶ 查看 | 查看制动器 | 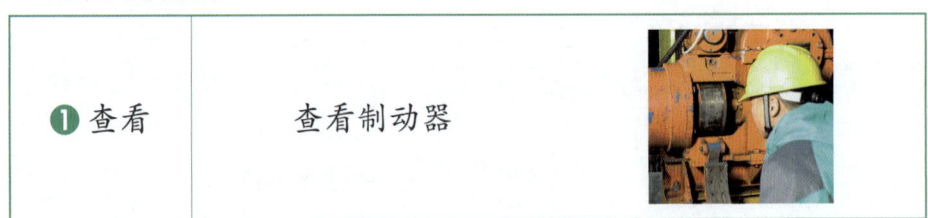 |

第 13 课 ｜ 测量制动器间隙

❷ 完全	完全贴合	
❸ 上端	制动器上端间隙	
❹ 下端	制动器下端间隙	

学习课文 Text 🎧 13-02

测量 制动器 间隙
Cèliáng zhìdòngqì jiànxì

先 释放 机械能，在 制动器 关闭 时，查看
制动衬 和 制动鼓，确认 制动衬 是否 可以 完全
贴合 制动鼓。在 制动器 打开 时，用 塞尺 测量
制动衬 和 制动鼓 之间 的 间隙。间隙 不大于 0.7[①]

---
① 0.7 读作"零点七"（líng diǎn qī）。

háomǐ, zhìdòngchèn shàngduān hé xiàduān de jiànxì xiāngtóng, zé fúhé yāoqiú.
毫米，制动衬 上端 和 下端 的 间隙 相同，则 符合要求。

Measure the Clearances of the Brake

First, release the mechanical energy. When the brake is locked, check the brake lining and the brake drum to find out if the brake lining can completely fit the brake drum. When the brake is turned on, measure the clearance between the brake lining and the brake drum with a feeler gauge. It meets the requirements if the clearance is not more than 0.7 mm, and the clearance between the upper and lower ends of the brake lining is the same.

课文练习 Text Exercises

1. 选词填空。Choose the words to fill in the blanks.

① 测量制动器间隙是测量制动衬和（　　）之间的间隙。

　　A. 制动鼓　　B. 上端

② 制动器关闭时，制动衬可以完全（　　）制动鼓。

　　A. 贴合　　B. 关闭

③ 使用（　　）测量制动器间隙。　　A. 直尺　　B. 塞尺

④ 塞尺测量的间隙（　　）0.7 毫米。　　A. 不大于　　B. 不小于

2. 判断对错。Tell whether the following statements are true (T) or false (F).

① 测量制动器间隙前要释放机械能。　　（　　）

② 在制动器关闭时，制动衬要完全贴合制动鼓。　　（　　）

3 制动衬和制动鼓之间的间隙要不大于0.7毫米。　　　　（　　）

4 制动衬上端和下端的间隙要不大于0.7毫米。　　　　（　　）

学习语法 Grammar

语法点1 Grammar Point 1

能愿动词"可以"　The Optative Verb "可以"

"可以" indicates a possibility or capability. Its negative form is "不能". For example,

例句	英文翻译
Quèrèn zhìdòngchèn kěyǐ wánquán tiēhé zhìdònggǔ. 确认 制动衬 可以 完全 贴合 制动鼓。	Make sure that the brake lining completely fits the brake drum.
Diàntīgōng kěyǐ wéibǎo diàntī. 电梯工 可以 维保 电梯。	The elevator worker can maintain the elevator.
Sānjiǎo yàoshi kěyǐ dǎkāi céngmén. 三角 钥匙 可以 打开 层门。	The triangle key can be used to open the landing door.

连词成句。Rearrange the words into sentences.

1 ①清理　②抹布　③灰尘　④可以　⑤用
→ _____

2 ①阻止　②轿厢　③进入　④乘客　⑤护栏　⑥可以
→ _____

3 ①测量　②可以　③电压　④万用表
→ _____

4 ①电梯工　②救　③乘客　④可以
→ _____

语法点 2 Grammar Point 2

连词"则" The Conjunction "则"

"则" is used in written Chinese to indicate the sequence or the cause and effect between two words, phrases, or sentences. For example,

例句	英文翻译
Zhìdòngchèn kěyǐ wánquán tiēhé zhìdònggǔ, zé fúhé yāoqiú. 制动衬 可以 完全 贴合 制动鼓，则 符合 要求。	If the brake lining can completely fit the brake drum, (then) it meets the requirements.
Jiànxì bú dàyú 0.7 háomǐ, zé fúhé yāoqiú. 间隙 不 大于 0.7 毫米，则 符合 要求。	If the clearance is not more than 0.7mm, (then) it meets the requirements.
Shàngduān hé xiàduān de jiànxì xiāngtóng, zé fúhé yāoqiú. 上端 和 下端 的 间隙 相同，则 符合 要求。	If clearances at the upper and lower ends are the same, (then) it meets the requirements.

改写句子。 Rewrite the sentences.

1. 销轴没有锈迹，符合要求。
   _____ 则 _____ 。

2. 弹簧没有断裂，符合要求。
   _____ 则 _____ 。

3. 轿厢里面没有乘客，再断开电源。
   _____ 则 _____ 。

4. 松开制动器，对重开始下行。
   _____ 则 _____ 。

汉字书写 Writing Chinese Characters

职业拓展 Career Insight

电动升降机 Electric Elevator

In 1880, Werner von Siemens presented the world's first electric elevator at the Mannheim Trade Fair. Its external platform can take four passengers to the 20-meter-high temporary observation tower. The elevator was equipped with an electric motor under the platform and ran with the gear. This was another pioneering achievement of Siemens after its groundbreaking inventions—generators and electric railways. The idea of using electric motors to supply power to elevators and their rotating platforms first appeared in 1879, but it took

Siemens a year to realize this idea. Although it was behind the schedule, the project was completed towards the end of the fair and caused a sensation.

 小结 Summary

词语 Words

朗读下列词语。Read aloud the following words.

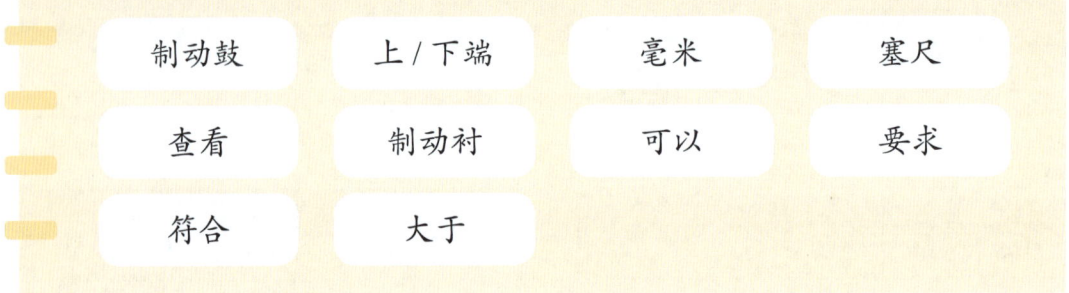

制动鼓	上 / 下端	毫米	塞尺
查看	制动衬	可以	要求
符合	大于		

语法 Grammar

朗读下列句子。Read aloud the following sentences.

1. 确认制动衬是否可以完全贴合制动鼓。
2. 三角钥匙可以打开层门。
3. 间隙不大于 0.7 毫米，则符合要求。
4. 制动衬上端和下端的间隙相同，则符合要求。

第13课 测量制动器间隙

课文理解 Text Comprehension

复述课文内容。Retell the text.

1. 先释放……，在……时，查看……，确认……制动鼓。
2. 在……时，用塞尺……和……的间隙。
3. 间隙不大于……，制动衬……和……相同，则符合要求。

第 14 课
Lesson 14

进入轿厢 (Jìnrù jiāoxiāng)
Get into the Elevator Car

复习 Revision

根据上一课课文选图填空。Choose the pictures to fill in the blanks based on the previous text.

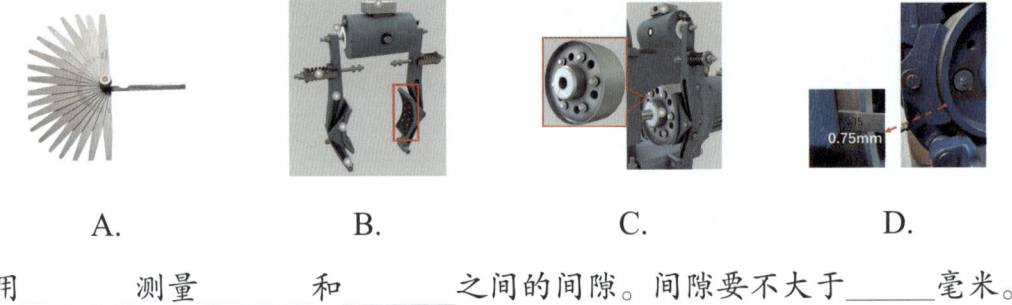

A.　　　　　B.　　　　　C.　　　　　D.

用_____测量_____和_____之间的间隙。间隙要不大于_____毫米。

热身 Warm-up

根据图片选择词语。Choose the words based on the pictures.

（　）　　　　　（　）　　　　　（　）

第14课 | 进入轿厢

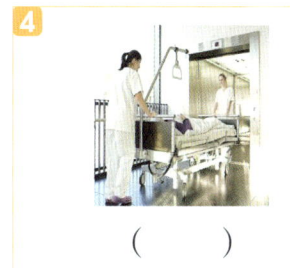 ④ (　)
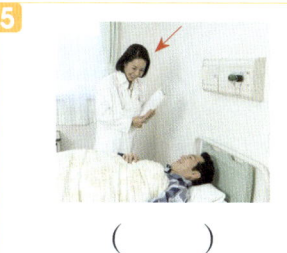 ⑤ (　)
 ⑥ (　)

A. 乘客电梯 chéngkè diàntī
passenger elevator

B. 轿门 jiàomén
elevator car door

C. 医护人员 yīhù rényuán
medical staff

D. 轿壁 jiàobì
elevator car wall

E. 轿底 jiàodǐ
elevator car platform

F. 病床电梯 bìngchuáng diàntī
bed elevator

 **学习生词 Words and Expressions** 🎧 14-01

1	轿底	jiàodǐ	*n.*	elevator car platform
2	轿壁	jiàobì	*n.*	elevator car wall
3	轿门	jiàomén	*n.*	elevator car door
4	部件	bùjiàn	*n.*	part
5	通常	tōngcháng	*adv.*	usually
6	病床	bìngchuáng	*n.*	hospital bed
7	窄	zhǎi	*adj.*	narrow
8	而	ér	*conj.*	and
9	长	cháng	*adj.*	long
10	医护人员	yīhù rényuán	*phr.*	medical staff

121

11	同时	tóngshí	n.	in the meantime, (at the) same time
12	宽	kuān	adj.	wide
13	短	duǎn	adj.	short
14	快速	kuàisù	adj.	fast, quick
15	进出	jìnchū	v.	get in and out

词语练习 Word Exercises

1. 认读词语。Recognize and read the words.

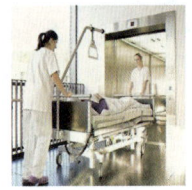  

病床电梯　　　　　　　轿底　　　　　　　　　轿门

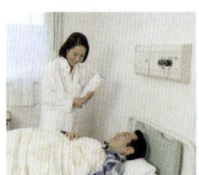  

医护人员　　　　　　　乘客电梯　　　　　　　轿壁

2. 朗读词语搭配。Read aloud the word collocations.

❶ 轿厢	长而窄的轿厢	
		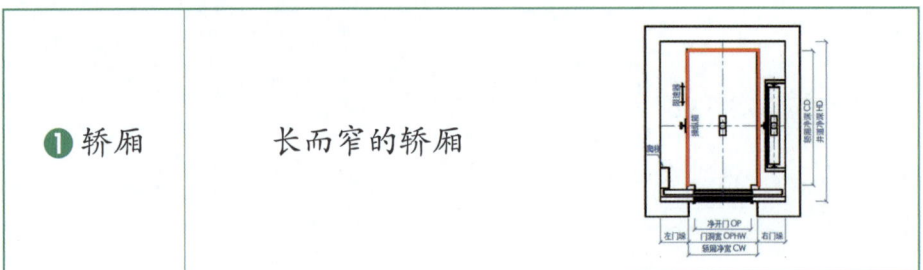

第14课 | 进入轿厢

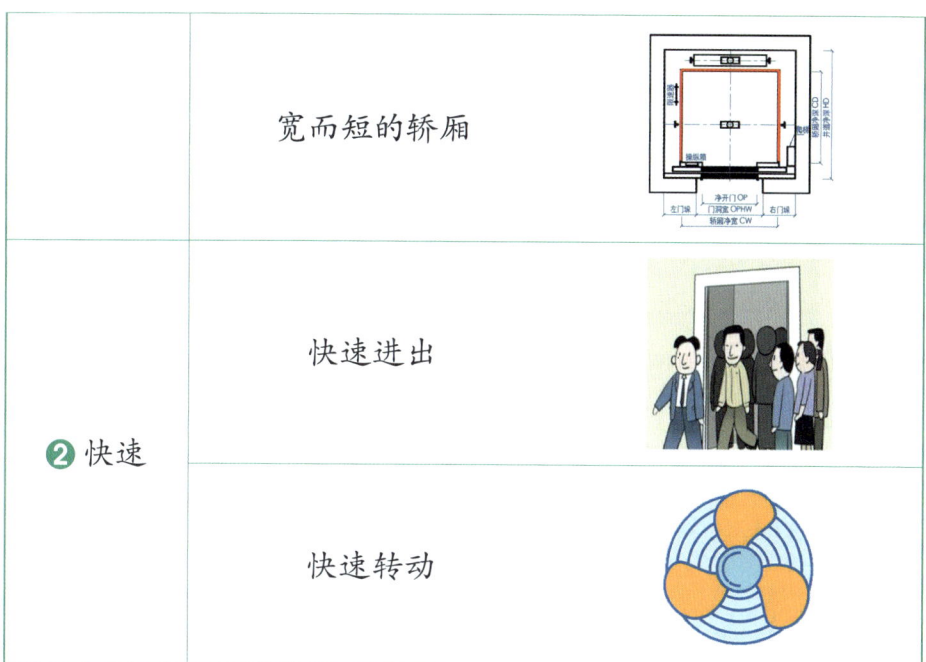

	宽而短的轿厢	
❷ 快速	快速进出	
	快速转动	

学习课文 Text 🎧 14-02

进入 轿厢
Jìnrù jiàoxiāng

轿厢 由 轿底、轿壁、轿门 等 部件 组成。

通常，病床 电梯 的 轿厢 窄 而 长，医护人员 和 病床 能 同时 进入。乘客电梯 的 轿厢 宽 而 短，乘客 能 快速 进出。

Get into the Elevator Car

The elevator car consists of a car platform, car walls, a car door and other parts. Usually, the bed elevator has a narrow and long car so that it can accommodate both the medical staff and the hospital bed. However, the car of the passenger elevator is wide and short for quick access.

课文练习 Text Exercises

1. 判断对错。Tell whether the following statements are true (T) or false (F).

    ① 乘客电梯和病床电梯的轿厢是相同的。　　　　　　　　　　（　　）
    ② 乘客电梯的轿厢窄而长。　　　　　　　　　　　　　　　　（　　）
    ③ 轿厢都有轿壁、轿底和轿门。　　　　　　　　　　　　　　（　　）
    ④ 医护人员不能进入病床电梯的轿厢。　　　　　　　　　　　（　　）

2. 选词填空。Choose the words to fill in the blanks.

    ① 轿底、轿壁、（　　）等部件组成轿厢。
       A. 轿门　　　　　　B. 层门　　　　　　C. 电源
    ② 轿厢窄而长的是（　　）。
       A. 乘客电梯　　　　B. 病床电梯
    ③ 乘客电梯的轿厢宽而（　　）。
       A. 窄　　　　　　　B. 长　　　　　　　C. 短
    ④ 乘客能快速（　　）乘客电梯。
       A. 进出　　　　　　B. 清理　　　　　　C. 确认

第 14 课 | 进入轿厢

学习语法 Grammar

语法点 1 Grammar Point 1

频率副词"通常" The Adverb of Frequency "通常"

"通常" is a commonly-used adverb of frequency, indicating that a certain behavior or situation occurs in general circumstances.

例句	英文翻译
Tōngcháng, bìngchuáng diàntī de jiàoxiāng zhǎi ér cháng. **通常**，病床 电梯的 轿厢 窄而 长。	Usually, the bed elevator has a narrow and long car.
Tōngcháng, chéngkè diàntī de jiàoxiāng kuān ér duǎn. **通常**，乘客 电梯的 轿厢 宽 而 短。	Usually, the car of the passenger elevator is wide and short.
Tōngcháng, wéibǎo diàntī zhīqián, yào xiān dài ānquánmào. **通常**，维保电梯之前，要 先 戴安全帽。	Usually, one has to wear a safety helmet before the elevator maintenance.

连词成句。Rearrange the words into sentences.

1. ①通常 ②盘车救援 ③断开 ④要 ⑤电源 ⑥前
→ _____

2. ①锁上 ②电源 ③通常 ④断开 ⑤要 ⑥电源盒 ⑦先
→ _____

3. ①电梯 ②通常 ③准备 ④维保 ⑤要 ⑥工具
→ _____

4. ①盘车救援 ②口号 ③通常 ④喊 ⑤一起 ⑥要
→ _____

语法点 2 Grammar Point 2

连词"而" The Conjunction "而"

"而" indicates connection or addition. For example,

例句	英文翻译
Bìngchuáng diàntī de jiàoxiāng zhǎi ér cháng. 病床 电梯 的 轿厢 窄而 长。	The bed elevator has a narrow and long car.
Chéngkè diàntī de jiàoxiāng kuān ér duǎn. 乘客电梯的 轿厢 宽而 短。	The car of the passenger elevator is wide and short.
Jiùyuán chéngkè yào kuàisù ér ānquán. 救援 乘客 要 快速而安全。	Rescuing passengers needs to be quick and safe.

选词填空。Choose the words to fill in the blanks.

1. 乘客电梯的轿厢宽（　　）短。　　A. 而　　B. 或者
2. 电梯困人（　　）有故障时，要进行盘车救援。　　A. 而　　B. 或者
3. 病床电梯轿厢窄（　　）长。　　A. 而　　B. 或者
4. 按上行按钮（　　）下行按钮，电梯可以运行。　　A. 而　　B. 或者

汉字书写 Writing Chinese Characters

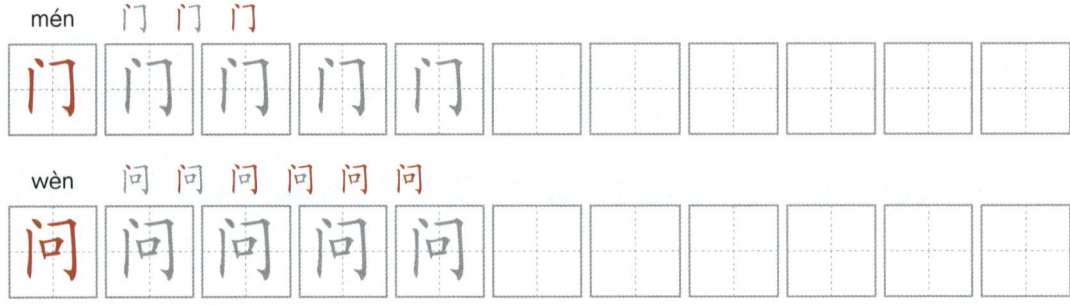

第14课 | 进入轿厢

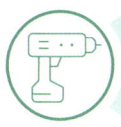 文化拓展 Culture Insight

鸟巢 National Stadium (Bird's Nest)

The National Stadium is located in Beijing and resembles a huge silver bird's nest. From a distance, it skillfully interweaves steel elements and forms an architectural masterpiece full of artistic charm. Walking into the National Stadium, people are shocked by its scale and technology, as if the designer's intelligence has penetrated into the whole interior space. As night falls, the National Stadium shines brightly and looks like a bright pearl shining in the night. It is the venue for the opening and closing ceremonies of the 2008 Beijing Olympic Games and a landmark of Beijing.

小结 Summary

词语 Words

朗读下列词语。Read aloud the following words.

轿壁	轿门	轿底	长
短	而	乘客电梯	病床电梯
宽	窄		

语法 Grammar

朗读下列句子。Read aloud the following sentences.

1. 通常，病床电梯的轿厢窄而长。
2. 通常，维保电梯前，要先戴安全帽。
3. 通常，乘客电梯的轿厢宽而短。
4. 救援乘客要快速而安全。

课文理解 Text Comprehension

复述课文内容。Retell the text.

1. 轿厢由……等部件组成。
2. 通常，病床电梯的……，……和……同时进入。
3. 乘客电梯的轿厢……，乘客能……。

第 15 课 Lesson 15

Chákàn jiàoxiāng zhàomíng 查看轿厢照明
Inspect the Lighting of the Elevator Car

复习 Revision

根据图片选择词语。Choose the words based on the pictures.

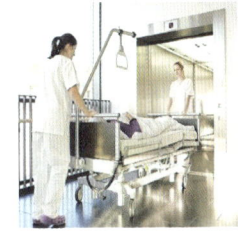

1 病床电梯（   ）
乘客电梯（   ）

2 轿壁（   ）
轿底（   ）

3 轿门（   ）
层门（   ）

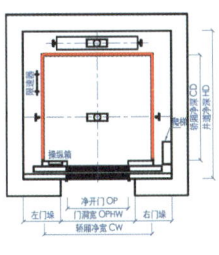

4 宽而短的轿厢（   ）
窄而长的轿厢（   ）

129

职通中文 电梯安装与维修保养（初级篇）

 热身 Warm-up

看图选词，将对应的字母填在括号里。Look at the pictures and choose the words. Put the corresponding letters in the brackets.

A.

B.

C.

D.

E.

F.

1	轿顶	jiàodǐng	car roof	(　　)
2	熄灭	xīmiè	extinguish	(　　)
3	供电	gōngdiàn	supply power	(　　)
4	照明	zhàomíng	light, illuminate	(　　)
5	小时	xiǎoshí	hour	(　　)
6	蓄电池	xùdiànchí	storage battery	(　　)

第 15 课 | 查看轿厢照明

 ## 学习生词 Words and Expressions 15-01

1	照明	zhàomíng	v.	light, illuminate
2	熄灭	xīmiè	v.	extinguish
3	除了	chúle	prep.	in addition to
4	还	hái	adv.	also
5	应急	yìng//jí	v.	meet an emergent need
6	轿顶	jiàodǐng	n.	elevator car roof
7	蓄电池	xùdiànchí	n.	storage battery
8	给	gěi	prep.	for
9	供电	gōngdiàn	v.	supply power
10	此时	cǐshí	n.	at this moment
11	小时	xiǎoshí	n.	hour

词语练习 Word Exercises

1. 认读词语。Recognize and read the words.

轿顶

蓄电池

供电

小时　　　　　　　　熄灭　　　　　　　　照明

2. 朗读词语搭配。Read aloud the word collocations.

❶ 轿顶	进入轿顶	
❷ 供电	供电电源	
❸ 熄灭	照明熄灭	
❹ 照明	轿厢照明	
	应急照明	

 学习课文 Text 🎧 15-02

查看 轿厢 照明
Chákàn jiàoxiāng zhàomíng

打开 机房 电源盒，断开 曳引机 电源，观察 轿厢 照明 是否 熄灭。电梯 轿厢 里 除了 轿厢 照明，还有 应急照明。断开 轿厢 照明 电源，轿顶 上 的 蓄电池 给 应急 照明 供电，此时，应急 照明 能 0.5① 小时 不 熄灭。

Inspect the Lighting of the Elevator Car

Open the power box in the machine room, and disconnect the power to the traction machine to see if the car lighting is extinguished. In addition to the car lighting, emergency lighting is also available in the elevator car. Disconnect the power supply of the car lighting, and the storage supply on the car roof can supply power to the emergency lighting. The emergency lighting will stay on for half an hour at this moment.

---

① 0.5 读作"零点五"（líng diǎn wǔ）。

课文练习 Text Exercises

1. 判断对错。Tell whether the following statements are true (T) or false (F).

   ① 检查轿厢照明要断开曳引机电源。（　　）
   ② 轿厢里有轿厢照明和应急照明。（　　）
   ③ 轿厢应急照明能用 0.5 小时。（　　）
   ④ 轿顶上有蓄电池。（　　）

2. 选词填空。Choose the words to fill in the blanks.

   ① 打开机房电源盒，（　　）曳引机电源。　A. 断开　　B. 打开
   ② 检查应急照明，要断开（　　）的电源。
   　　　　　　　　　　　　　　　A. 应急照明　B. 轿厢照明
   ③ 轿顶蓄电池给应急照明（　　）。　A. 熄灭　　B. 供电
   ④ 除了要检查轿厢照明，还有（　　）照明。
   　　　　　　　　　　　　　　　A. 应急　　B. 正常

学习语法 Grammar

语法点1 Grammar Point 1

除了……

"除了……" is used to indicate extra things. It is usually followed by "还", "也", and "都"。"除了……（以外）" can also be used. For example,

例句	英文翻译
Jiàoxiāng lǐmiàn, chúle jiàoxiāng zhàomíng, hái yǒu yìngjí zhàomíng. 轿厢 里面，除了 轿厢 照明，还有 应急 照明。	In addition to the car lighting, emergency lighting is also available in the elevator car.

第15课 | 查看轿厢照明

（续表）

例句	英文翻译
Jīfáng lǐmiàn, chúle diàntīgōng A, hái yǒu diàntīgōng B. 机房里面，除了电梯工 A，还有电梯工 B。	Besides elevator worker A, elevator worker B is also in the machine room.
Wéibǎo diàntī qián, chúle yào chuān gōngzuòfú, hái yào dài ānquánmào. 维保电梯前，除了要穿工作服，还要戴安全帽。	Besides the safety helmet, one also needs to wear work clothes before the elevator maintenance.

改写句子。Rewrite the sentences.

1 电梯工要穿工作服，要戴安全帽。

　　_____除了_____，还_____。

2 电梯工 A 和电梯工 B 都进入了机房。

　　除了_____，_____也_____。

3 检查曳引机时，要用耳朵听，要用眼睛看。

　　_____除了_____，还_____。

4 我是电梯工，他们都不是电梯工。

　　除了_____，他们都_____。

语法点 2 Grammar Point 2

介词"给" The Preposition "给"

"给" is followed by the object of an action. It is used in the sentence structure "给 + Noun + Phrasal Verb". For example,

例句	英文翻译
Diàntīgōng gěi jiǎnsùxiāng gēnghuàn rùnhuáyóu le. 电梯工给减速箱更换润滑油了。	The elevator worker replaces lubricant for the reduction gearbox.

135

（续表）

例句	英文翻译
Yòng mābù gěi yuánjiàn qīnglǐ huīchén. 用 抹布 给 元件 清理 灰尘。	Remove dust from the components with a duster.
Xùdiànchí gěi yìngjí zhàomíng gōngdiàn. 蓄电池 给 应急 照明 供电。	The storage battery can supply power for the emergency lighting.

连词成句。Rearrange the words into sentences.

1 ①照明　②给　③蓄电池　④供电　⑤应急
→ _____

2 ①电梯工　②我　③戴　④给　⑤要　⑥安全帽
→ _____

3 ①蓄电池　②轿厢　③给　④电梯工　⑤更换
→ _____

4 ①轿厢　②放上　③我　④里面　⑤给　⑥护栏　⑦了
→ _____

 汉字书写 Writing Chinese Characters

niú
牛 牛 牛 牛
牛 牛 牛 牛 牛

shēng
生 生 生 生 生
生 生 生 生 生

zhū
朱 朱 朱 朱 朱 朱
朱 朱 朱 朱 朱

第15课 | 查看轿厢照明

zhū
株 株 株 株 株 株 株 株 株 株 株
株 株 株 株 株

职业拓展 Career Insight

新中国第一部电梯 The First Elevator in New China

The earliest elevator in New China is still working in Shanghai today. The first home-made elevator was manufactured by Tianjin Congqingsheng Electric Machinery Factory in 1951. In September 1959, the joint state-private enterprise Shanghai Elevator Factory manufactured and installed 81 elevators and 4 escalators for the Great Hall of the People in Beijing and other major national projects. The four escalators (AC2-59 model) have historical significance as they are the milestones in China's independent manufacturing of elevators. They were co-developed by Shanghai Elevator Factory and Shanghai Jiao Tong University, and were finally installed at Beijing Railway Station.

小结 Summary

 词语 Words

朗读下列词语。Read aloud the following words.

| 给 | 应急 | 小时 | 此时 |
| 照明 | 除了 | 蓄电池 | 还 |

语法 Grammar

朗读下列句子。Read aloud the following sentences.

1. 电梯工给减速箱更换润滑油了。
2. 蓄电池给应急照明供电。
3. 维保电梯前除了要穿工作服，还要戴安全帽。
4. 轿厢里面，除了轿厢照明，还有应急照明。

课文理解 Text Comprehension

复述课文内容。Retell the text.

1. 打开机房……，断开……，观察……。
2. 电梯轿厢里除了……，还有……。
3. 断开……电源，轿顶上的……给……，此时，……不熄灭。

第 16 课 Lesson 16
Cèshì bàojǐng gōngnéng
测试报警功能
Test the Alarm Function

复习 Revision

朗读下列词语。Read aloud the following words.

| 给 | 应急 | 小时 | 此时 |
| 照明 | 除了 | 蓄电池 | 还有 |

热身 Warm-up

看图选词，将对应的字母填在括号里。Look at the pictures and choose the words. Put the corresponding letters in the brackets.

A.　　　　　　　　B.　　　　　　　　C.

139

D.   E.   F.

1	报警按钮	bàojǐng ànniǔ	alarm button	( )
2	机房电话	jīfáng diànhuà	the phone of the machine room	( )
3	轿厢电话	jiàoxiāng diànhuà	the phone of the elevator car	( )
4	监控室	jiānkòngshì	monitor room	( )
5	铃声	língshēng	alert tone	( )
6	通话口	tōnghuàkǒu	intercom speaker	( )

学习生词 Words and Expressions  16-01

1	报警	bào//jǐng	v.	(give an) alarm
2	功能	gōngnéng	n.	function
3	监控室	jiānkòngshì	n.	monitor room
4	后	hòu	n.	after
5	报警按钮	bàojǐng ànniǔ	phr.	alarm button
6	通话口	tōnghuàkǒu	n.	intercom speaker
7	铃声	língshēng	n.	alert tone

8	接	jiē	v.	answer (the telephone)
9	电话	diànhuà	n.	phone
10	彼此	bǐcǐ	pron.	each other
11	清楚	qīngchu	adj.	clear
12	地	de	part.	used after an adjective/a phrase to form an adverbial adjunct before the verb
13	讲话	jiǎng//huà	v.	say
14	结束	jiéshù	v.	end

词语练习 Word Exercises

1. 认读词语。Recognize and read the words.

监控室

机房电话

轿厢电话

报警按钮

铃声

通话口

2. 朗读词语搭配。Read aloud the word collocations.

❶ 接	接电话	
❷ 按下	按下报警按钮	
❸ 监控室	查看监控室	
❹ 听到	听到铃声	

学习课文　Text　🎧 16-02

Cèshì bàojǐng gōngnéng
测试 报警 功能

Diàntīgōng A jìnrù jīfáng huò jiānkòngshì, diàntīgōng B
电梯工 A 进入 机房 或 监控室，电梯工 B
jìnrù jiàoxiāng. Zài jiàomén guānbì hòu, diàntīgōng B ànxia
进入 轿厢。在 轿门 关闭 后，电梯工 B 按下
bàojǐng ànniǔ, tōnghuàkǒu yǒu língshēng. Diàntīgōng A zài jīfáng
报警 按钮，通话口 有 铃声。电梯工 A 在 机房

第 16 课 | 测试报警功能

huò jiānkòngshì tīngdào língshēng hòu, jiē diànhuà. Quèrèn bǐcǐ dōu
或 监控室 听到 铃声 后，接 电话。确认 彼此 都
néng qīngchu de tīngdào jiǎnghuà hòu, cèshì jiéshù.
能 清楚 地 听到 讲话 后，测试 结束。

Test the Alarm Function

Elevator worker A enters the machine room or monitor room, and elevator worker B enters the elevator car. After closing the door, elevator worker B presses the alarm button and the alert tone rings at the intercom speaker. Elevator worker A in the machine room or monitor room answers the phone after hearing the alert tone. The test ends if both can hear each other's voice clearly.

课文练习 Text Exercises

1. 判断对错。Tell whether the following statements are true (T) or false (F).

   ① 测试报警功能时，机房和监控室都要测试。　　　　（　　）
   ② 监控室和轿厢都能清楚地听到彼此讲话后，测试结束。（　　）
   ③ 按报警按钮后，监控室和机房能通话。　　　　　　（　　）
   ④ 按报警按钮后，轿厢里面说话，监控室能听到。　　（　　）

2. 选词填空。Choose the words to fill in the blanks.

   ① 报警按钮在（　　）里面。
   　A. 层门　　　　　B. 机房　　　　　C. 轿厢
   ② 测试报警功能由（　　）电梯工进行。
   　A. 3 个　　　　　B. 2 个　　　　　C. 4 个

143

3 在（　　）听到铃声后，要接电话。

　A. 轿厢　　　　　　B. 电梯　　　　　　C. 机房

4 当电梯困人时，乘客要按（　　）。

　A. 报警按钮　　　　B. 下行按钮

学习语法 Grammar

语法点1 Grammar Point 1

结果补语　Resultative Complement

A resultative complement is used after a verb to show the result of an action. It is usually used in the sentence structure "Verb + Resultative Complement + Object" or "把 + Object + Verb + Resultative Complement". For example,

例句	英文翻译
Diàntīgōng A jìnrù jīfáng qián, bǎ hùlán fànghǎo. 电梯工 A 进入机房前，把护栏放好。	Elevator worker A first put the guard rail in place, and then entered the machine room.
Zài jiàoxiāng li, ànxia bàojǐng ànniǔ, wǒ néng tīngdào língshēng. 在 轿厢 里，按下 报警 按钮，我 能 听到 铃声。	Press the alarm button in the elevator car, and I can hear the alert tone.
Zài jīfáng, tīngdào língshēng de shíhou, jiētōng diànhuà. 在 机房，听到 铃声 的 时候，接通 电话。	Answer the phone in the machine room after hearing the alert tone.

选词填空。**Choose the words to fill in the blanks.**

1. 我能听_____他的声音。
   A. 到　　　　　B. 下　　　　　C. 上　　　　　D. 入

2. 电梯困人时，乘客按_____报警按钮。
   A. 到　　　　　B. 下　　　　　C. 上　　　　　D. 入

3. 维保电梯以前，电梯工要穿_____绝缘鞋。
   A. 到　　　　　B. 下　　　　　C. 上　　　　　D. 入

4. 开始工作以前，电梯工要先进_____机房。
   A. 到　　　　　B. 下　　　　　C. 上　　　　　D. 入

语法点 2　Grammar Point 2

代词"彼此"　The Pronoun "彼此"

"彼此" refers to two parties with mutual actions, feelings, or interactions. It can be translated as "each other" or "one another". For example,

例句	英文翻译
Cèshì bàojǐng shí, quèrèn bǐcǐ dōu néng qīngchu de tīngdào shēngyīn. 测试报警时，确认彼此都能清楚地听到声音。	Make sure both can clearly hear each other's voice in an alarm test.
Wǒ hé tā dōu néng tīngdào bǐcǐ de shēngyīn. 我和他都能听到彼此的声音。	He and I can hear each other's voice.
Wǒ hé tā bǐcǐ dōu bú rènshi. 我和他彼此都不认识。	We don't know each other.

改写句子。Rewrite the sentences.

1. 工作时，我们都要注意安全。
   ＿＿＿＿＿＿＿＿＿＿彼此＿＿＿＿＿＿＿＿＿＿。

2. 我认识他，他也认识我。
   ＿＿＿＿＿＿＿＿＿＿彼此＿＿＿＿＿＿＿＿＿＿。

3. 我能听到他的声音，他也能听到我的声音。
   ＿＿＿＿＿＿＿＿＿＿彼此＿＿＿＿＿＿＿＿＿＿。

4. 我是电梯工，他是电梯工。
   ＿＿＿＿＿＿＿＿＿＿彼此＿＿＿＿＿＿＿＿＿＿。

 汉字书写 Writing Chinese Characters

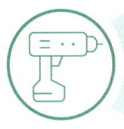# 文化拓展 Culture Insight

算盘 Abacus

Abacus is a tool used for calculation, which is usually made of wood with small wooden sticks fixed inside. These wooden sticks are adorned with wooden beads and divided into upper and lower parts. In general, each bead in the upper part represents 5, and each bead in the lower part represents 1. The abacus has different operating principles and can be used not only for decimal operations but also for hexadecimal operations. Although the abacus has been largely replaced by computers, it is still used in some parts of Asia and the Middle East.

# 小结 Summary

 词语 Words

朗读下列词语。Read aloud the following words.

报警	功能	通话口	结束
接	发出	电话	彼此
铃声	监控室		

语法 Grammar

朗读下列句子。Read aloud the following sentences.

1. 在机房，听到铃声的时候，接通电话。
2. 按下报警按钮，我能听到铃声。
3. 测试报警功能时，确认彼此都能清楚地听到声音。
4. 我和他彼此都不认识。

课文理解 Text Comprehension

复述课文内容。Retell the text.

1. 电梯工 A……，电梯工 B……。
2. 在轿门……，电梯工 B 按下……，通话口……。
3. 电梯工 A 在……后，接……。
4. 确认……后，……。

第 17 课 Lesson 17

Guānchá jǐngdào bùjiàn
观察井道部件
Observe the Components in the Hoistway

 复习 Revision

根据图片选择词语。Choose the words based on the pictures.

1. 监控室（　　）
   机房（　　）

2. 铃声（　　）
   讲话（　　）

3. 轿厢电话（　　）
   机房电话（　　）

4. 按报警按钮（　　）
   按电话按钮（　　）

149

热身 Warm-up

看图选词，将对应的字母填在括号里。Look at the pictures and choose the words. Put the corresponding letters in the brackets.

A. 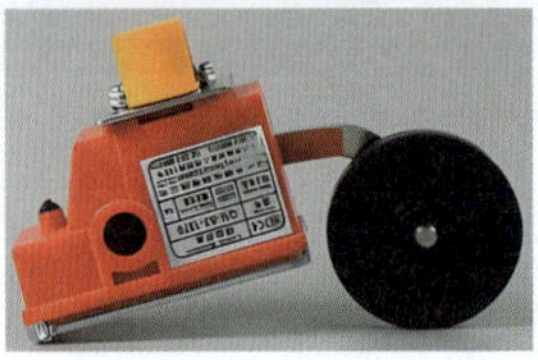　　　　　　　B. 　　　　　　　C.

D. 　　　　　　　E. 　　　　　　　F.

1. 补偿链　　　bǔchángliàn　　　compensation chain　　　(　)
2. 随行电缆　　suíxíng diànlǎn　　trailing cable　　　　　(　)
3. 井道　　　　jǐngdào　　　　　hoistway　　　　　　　(　)
4. 张紧轮　　　zhāngjǐnlún　　　tension pully　　　　　 (　)
5. 导轨　　　　dǎoguǐ　　　　　guide rail　　　　　　 (　)
6. 极限开关　　jíxiàn kāiguān　　final limit switch　　　 (　)

第 17 课 | 观察井道部件

学习生词 Words and Expressions 🎧 17-01

1	井道	jǐngdào	n.	hoistway
2	学生	xuéshēng	n.	student
3	哪些	nǎxiē	pron.	what
4	老师	lǎoshī	n.	teacher
5	随行电缆	suíxíng diànlǎn	phr.	trailing cable
6	补偿链	bǔchángliàn	n.	compensation chain
7	其他	qítā	pron.	else
8	需要	xūyào	opt.	need
9	吗	ma	part.	*used at the end of a question*
10	导轨	dǎoguǐ	n.	guide rail
11	最	zuì	adv.	to the highest/lowest degree
12	上方	shàngfāng	n.	top
13	极限开关	jíxiàn kāiguān	phr.	final limit switch
14	限位开关	xiànwèi kāiguān	phr.	limit switch
15	下方	xiàfāng	n.	bottom
16	张紧轮	zhāngjǐnlún	n.	tension pully

词语练习 Word Exercises

1. 认读词语。Recognize and read the words.

 井道

 随行电缆

 补偿链

 极限开关

 导轨

 张紧轮

2. 朗读词语搭配。Read aloud the word collocations.

❶ 导轨	检查导轨	
❷ 限位开关	按限位开关	
❸ 上方	轿厢最上方	
❹ 下方	轿厢最下方	

第 17 课 | 观察井道部件

学习课文 Text 🎧 17-02

观察 井道部件
Guānchá jǐngdào bùjiàn

学生：井道里面要检查哪些部件？
Xuéshēng: Jǐngdào lǐmiàn yào jiǎnchá nǎxiē bùjiàn?

老师：除了轿厢和对重，还有随行电缆、补偿链和层门。
Lǎoshī: Chúle jiàoxiāng hé duìzhòng, hái yǒu suíxíng diànlǎn, bǔchángliàn hé céngmén.

学生：还有其他需要检测的部件吗？
Xuéshēng: Hái yǒu qítā xūyào jiǎncè de bùjiàn ma?

老师：导轨最上方还有极限开关和限位开关，最下方还有缓冲器和张紧轮。
Lǎoshī: Dǎoguǐ zuì shàngfāng hái yǒu jíxiàn kāiguān hé xiànwèi kāiguān, zuì xiàfāng hái yǒu huǎnchōngqì hé zhāngjǐnlún.

Observe the Components in the Hoistway

Student: What components do we need to check in the hoistway?

Teacher: In addition to the elevator car and the counterweight, we also need to check the trailing cables, compensation chains, and landing door.

Student: What other components do we need to test?

Teacher: There is a final limit switch and a limit switch at the top of the guide rail, and two buffers and a tension pully at the bottom.

课文练习 Text Exercises

1. 判断对错。Tell whether the following statements are true (T) or false (F).

   ① 井道里面有轿厢、对重、随行电缆和补偿链。　　　　　（　　）
   ② 极限开关在导轨最上方。　　　　　　　　　　　　　　（　　）
   ③ 张紧轮在导轨最上方。　　　　　　　　　　　　　　　（　　）
   ④ 缓冲器和张紧轮不在井道里面。　　　　　　　　　　　（　　）

2. 选词填空。Choose the words to fill in the blanks.

   ① （　　）是井道里面的部件。　　　A. 层门　　　B. 曳引机
   ② 电梯轿厢在（　　）里面运行。　　A. 井道　　　B. 机房
   ③ 张紧轮在导轨的（　　）。　　　　A. 上方　　　B. 下方
   ④ 缓冲器在导轨的（　　）。　　　　A. 上方　　　B. 下方

学习语法 Grammar

语法点1 Grammar Point 1

副词"最" The Adverb "最"

"最" is used before a word of location to indicate the extreme point in a certain direction. For example,

例句	英文翻译
Dǎoguǐ zuì shàngfāng yǒu jíxiàn kāiguān. 导轨 最 上方 有 极限 开关。	The final limit switch is at the top of the guide rail.
Jǐngdào zuì xiàfāng yǒu huǎnchōngqì. 井道 最 下方 有 缓冲器。	The buffer is at the bottom of the hoistway.

例句	英文翻译
Jiàoxiāng zuì shàngfāng yǒu zhàomíng. 轿厢 最 上方 有 照明。	Lights are at the top of the elevator car.

连词成句。Rearrange the words into sentences.

 ①最 ②有 ③井道 ④上方 ⑤极限开关 → _____

② ①轿厢 ②有 ③最 ④护栏 ⑤里面 → _____

③ ①下方 ②导轨 ③最 ④有 ⑤张紧轮 → _____

④ ①缓冲器 ②最 ③井道 ④在 ⑤下方 → _____

语法点 2 Grammar Point 2

副词"还" The Adverb "还"

"还" is used before a verb to indicate somebody or something beyond a certain range. For example,

例句	英文翻译
Chúle jiàoxiāng hé duìzhòng, hái yǒu suíxíng diànlǎn. 除了 轿厢 和 对重，还有 随行 电缆。	Besides the elevator car and counterweight, there are also trailing cables.
Zuì shàngfāng yǒu jíxiàn kāiguān, hái yǒu xiànwèi kāiguān. 最 上方 有 极限 开关，还有 限位 开关。	There is not only a final limit switch, but also a limit switch at the top (of the guide rail).
Jǐngdào li yǒu jiàoxiāng, hái yǒu qítā bùjiàn ma? 井道 里 有 轿厢，还有 其他 部件 吗？	Besides the elevator car, are there any other components in the hoistway?

改写句子。Rewrite the sentences.

1. 电梯工要穿工作服,要戴安全帽。
   _____,还_____。

2. 导轨最上方有极限开关、限位开关。
   _____,还_____。

3. 检查曳引机时,要用耳朵听,要用眼睛看。
   _____,还_____。

4. 井道里面要检查层门,要检查对重。
   _____,还_____。

 汉字书写 Writing Chinese Characters

职业拓展 Career Insight

电梯自动平层系统 Automatic Leveling System for Elevators

The Automatic Leveling System is an apparatus designed to ensure that an elevator can precisely stop at each floor. It works through a mechanism where a 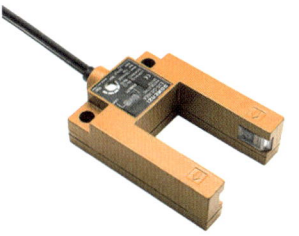 magnetic detector within the elevator car interacts with the unique leveling markers on each floor. Upon synchronization, the system confirms the elevator has leveled perfectly. The control system, responding to the chosen floor, calculates the elevator's position and speed with an encoder to adjust the motor's RPM to facilitate a smooth deceleration and landing at the desired floor. This can not only make passengers feel safe and comfortable, but also improve the elevator's traffic handling efficiency and help save energy.

小结 Summary

 词语 Words

朗读下列词语。Read aloud the following words.

导轨	其他	老师	井道
极限开关	什么	学生	下方
上方	补偿链		

语法 Grammar

朗读下列句子。Read aloud the following sentences.

1. 井道里除了轿厢和对重，还有随行电缆。
2. 井道里有轿厢，还有其他部件吗？
3. 导轨最上方有极限开关和限位开关。
4. 导轨最下方有缓冲器和张紧轮。

课文理解 Text Comprehension

复述课文内容。Retell the text.

1. 学生：……部件？
2. 老师：除了……，还有……、……和……。
3. 学生：还有……吗？
4. 老师：导轨最上方还有……，最下方还有……。

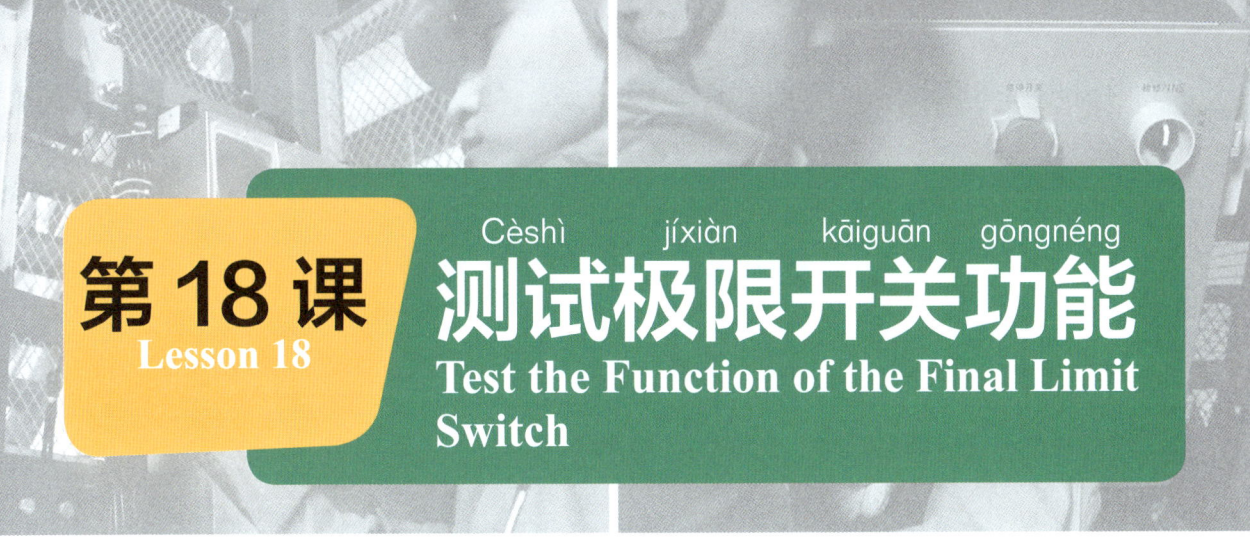

第 18 课 Lesson 18

Cèshì jíxiàn kāiguān gōngnéng
测试极限开关功能
Test the Function of the Final Limit Switch

 复习 Revision

根据图片选择词语。Choose the words based on the pictures.

❶ 导轨（　　）
　 工具（　　）

❷ 张紧轮（　　）
　 限速器（　　）

❸ 补偿链（　　　）
　 随行电缆（　　　）

❹ 机房（　　）
　 井道（　　）

159

 热身 Warm-up

看图选词，将对应的字母填在括号里。Look at the pictures and choose the words. Put the corresponding letters in the brackets.

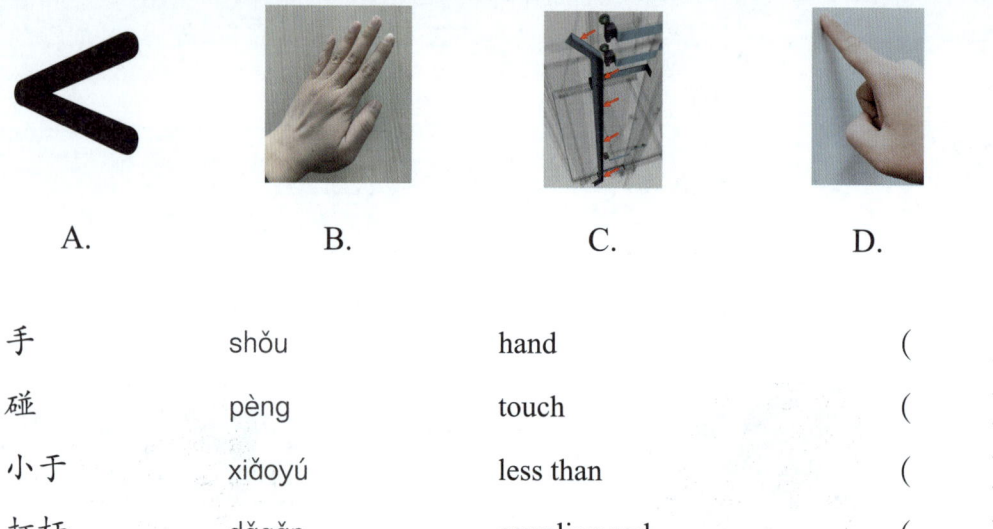

A.　　　　　　B.　　　　　　C.　　　　　　D.

1	手	shǒu	hand	( )
2	碰	pèng	touch	( )
3	小于	xiǎoyú	less than	( )
4	打杆	dǎgǎn	coupling rod	( )

 学习生词 Words and Expressions 🎧 18-01

1	向	xiàng	*prep.*	towards
2	直到	zhídào	*v.*	till
3	手	shǒu	*n.*	hand
4	碰	pèng	*v.*	touch
5	按住	ànzhù	*phr.*	press

6	分别	fēnbié	adv.	separately
7	应	yīng	opt.	should
8	顶楼	dǐnglóu	n.	top floor
9	打杆	dǎgǎn	n.	coupling rod
10	距离	jùlí	n.	distance, clearance
11	正常	zhèngcháng	adj.	normal
12	小于	xiǎoyú	v.	(be) less than
13	缓冲	huǎnchōng	v.	buffer

词语练习 Word Exercises

1. 认读词语。 Recognize and read the words.

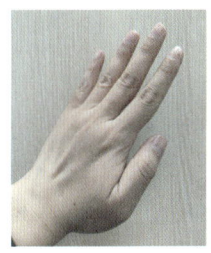
手

碰

按住

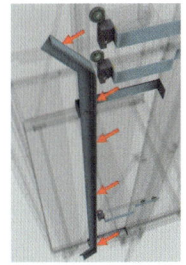
打杆

缓冲距离

小于

2. 朗读词语搭配。Read aloud the word collocations.

❶ 按住	按住极限开关	
❷ 小于	二小于六	
❸ 缓冲距离	测量缓冲距离	
❹ 碰	碰到按钮	

学习课文 Text 🎧 18-02

Cèshì　jíxiàn　kāiguān gōngnéng
测试 极限开关 功能

Lǎoshī　hé　xuéshēng　jìnrù　jiǎodǐng,　diàntī jiǎnxiū xiàng shàng
老师 和 学生 进入 轿顶，电梯检修 向 上

yùnxíng,　zhídào shǒu néng pèngdào jíxiàn kāiguān。Ànzhù　jíxiàn
运行，直到 手 能 碰到 极限 开关。按住 极限

第 18 课 | 测试极限开关功能

开关，分别检修上行和下行，电梯应不能运行。电梯检修运行到顶楼平层位置，测量极限开关和轿厢上打杆的距离，正常应小于对重缓冲距离。

Test the Function of the Final Limit Switch

The teacher and the student, both on the car roof, command the elevator to ascend till their hands can touch the final limit switch. The elevator won't travel if they press either the button "Up" or "Down", while still pressing and holding the final limit switch. As the elevator reaches the top landing floor, measure the distance between the final limit switch and the coupling rod on the car. The reading should be less than the counterweight's buffer clearance.

课文练习 Text Exercises

1. 判断对错。Tell whether the following statements are true (T) or false (F).

    1. 测试极限开关功能需要 2 个人。　　　　　　　　　　（　　）
    2. 按住极限开关，电梯能够检修运行。　　　　　　　　（　　）
    3. 在顶楼平层位置测量极限开关和打杆的距离。　　　　（　　）
    4. 极限开关和打杆的距离要小于对重缓冲距离。　　　　（　　）

2. 选词填空。Choose the words to fill in the blanks.

1. 极限开关要在（　　）进行测试。　　A. 机房　　B. 轿顶
2. 极限开关要在（　　）状态下进行测试。　A. 正常　　B. 检修
3. 按住极限开关，电梯（　　）移动。　　A. 不能　　B. 能
4. 老师要测量极限开关和（　　）的距离。　A. 轿厢上打杆　　B. 轿顶

学习语法 Grammar

语法点1 Grammar Point 1

介词"向"　The Preposition "向"

"向" indicates the direction, goal, or object of an action. A sentence usually goes like "向 + Noun + Verb Phrase". For example,

例句	英文翻译
Diàntī jiǎnxiū xiàng shàng yùnxíng. 电梯检修 向 上 运行。	The elevator travels upwards during the inspection.
Bǎ hùlán xiàng wài yídòng. 把护栏 向 外 移动。	Move the guard rail outward.
Diàntīgōng xiàng wǒ quèrèn wèizhì. 电梯工 向 我 确认 位置。	The elevator worker confirms the location with me.

连词成句。Rearrange the words into sentences.

1. ①向　②运行　③电梯　④检修　⑤上
   → _____

2. ①注入　②向　③润滑油　④电梯工　⑤里面　⑥减速箱
   → _____

3 ①蓄电池　②应急照明　③向　④供电

→ _____

4 ①电梯工　②井道　③向　④里面　⑤查看　⑥部件

→ _____

语法点 2　Grammar Point 2

能愿动词"应"　The Optative Verb "应"

It is mostly used in written Chinese to express obligation or duty. You can say "应该" in spoken Chinese. For example,

例句	英文翻译
Bèi kùn chéngkè yīng zài jiàoxiāng děngdài. 被困 乘客 应在 轿厢 等待。	The trapped riders should wait in the elevator car.
Dǎkāi céngmén yīng shǐyòng sānjiǎo yàoshi. 打开 层门 应 使用 三角 钥匙。	A triangle key should be used to open the landing door.
Wéibǎo diàntī yīng dài ānquánmào. 维保 电梯 应 戴 安全帽。	A safety helmet should be worn when maintaining the elevator.

选词填空。Choose the words to fill in the blanks.

1 按住极限开关，电梯不_____运行。　　A. 应　　B. 能

2 盘车救援时，电梯工_____一起喊口号。　A. 应　　B. 能

3 测量电压_____使用万用表。　　　　　A. 应　　B. 能

4 轿厢_____向下检修运行。　　　　　　A. 应　　B. 能

汉字书写 Writing Chinese Characters

文化拓展 Culture Insight

中国梦 Chinese Dream

Chinese Dream, a guiding principle and political vision proposed by President Xi Jinping, embodies the prospect of reviving the glory of Chinese nation. Its central tenets are to make the country prosperous, foster national vitality, and ensure the happiness of Chinese people. To realize Chinese Dream, we must adhere to the path of socialism with Chinese characteristics, carry forward Chinese spiritual heritage, and

consolidate the collective strength of Chinese nation. The strategies for realizing Chinese Dream involve coordinated progress in five realms: political, economic, cultural, social, and ecological systems. Chinese Dream is not only a dream for Chinese people, but also a dream for the globe, in some ways. It conveys Chinese people's pursuit of and contribution to the peace and development of the world.

小结 Summary

词语 Words

朗读下列词语。Read aloud the following words.

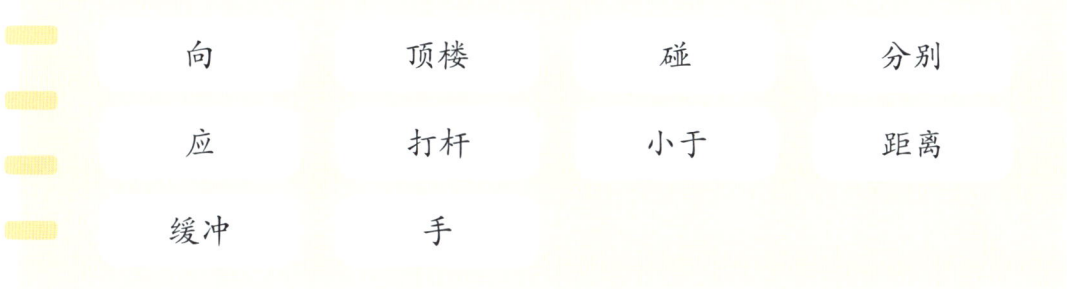

语法 Grammar

朗读下列句子。Read aloud the following sentences.

1. 把护栏向外移动。
2. 电梯检修向上运行。
3. 打开层门应使用三角钥匙。
4. 按住极限开关，电梯应不能运行。

课文理解 Text Comprehension

复述课文内容。Retell the text.

1. 老师和学生……，电梯检修……，直到……。
2. 按住……，分别……，电梯应……。
3. 电梯检修运行到……，测量……和……的距离，正常应……。

第 19 课 Lesson 19
检查导轨 Jiǎnchá dǎoguǐ
Inspect the Guide Rails

复习 Revision

朗读下列词语。Read aloud the following words.

向	顶楼	碰	分别
应	打杆	小于	距离
缓冲	手		

热身 Warm-up

看图连线。Look at the pictures and match them with the words.

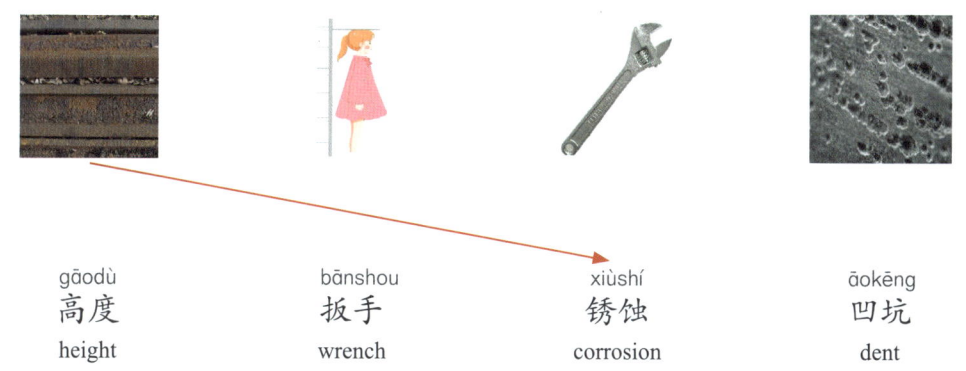

gāodù
高度
height

bānshou
扳手
wrench

xiùshí
锈蚀
corrosion

āokēng
凹坑
dent

学习生词 Words and Expressions 19-01

1	从	cóng	*prep.*	from
2	目测	mùcè	*v.*	check with one's eyes
3	变形	biàn//xíng	*v.*	deform
4	列	liè	*m.*	line
5	台阶	táijiē	*n.*	step
6	高度	gāodù	*n.*	height
7	表面	biǎomiàn	*n.*	surface
8	凹坑	āokēng	*n.*	dent
9	锈蚀	xiùshí	*v.*	corrode
10	对于	duìyú	*prep.*	for
11	连接板	liánjiēbǎn	*n.*	gusset
12	螺栓	luóshuān	*n.*	bolt
13	扳手	bānshou	*n.*	wrench
14	松动	sōngdòng	*v.*	loose

第 19 课 | 检查导轨

词语练习 Word Exercises

1. 认读词语。Recognize and read the words.

| 凹坑 | 锈蚀 | 螺栓 |

| 连接板 | 高度 | 扳手 |

2. 朗读词语搭配。Read aloud the word collocations.

❶ 表面	导轨表面	
❷ 高度	机房高度	
❸ 台阶	检查台阶	
❹ 松动	检查是否松动	

学习课文 Text 🎧 19-02

检查 导轨
Jiǎnchá dǎoguǐ

从 顶层 进入 轿顶，检修 下行，目测 导轨是否 变形；检查 各列 导轨 是否 有 台阶，台阶高度 不能 大于 0.05① 毫米；查看 导轨 表面 是否有 凹坑 和 锈蚀；对于 导轨 连接板 上 的 螺栓，用 扳手 检查 是否 松动。

Inspect the Guide Rails

Enter the elevator car roof from the top floor and travel downwards. Check with your eyes if the guide rails are deformed. Check if there is a height deviation between rails (the deviation should not exceed 0.05 mm). Check if there are dents and corrosion on the rails' surface, and check with a wrench if the bolts on the rail gussets have become loose.

---

① 0.05 读作"零点零五"（líng diǎn líng wǔ）。

课文练习 Text Exercises

1. 判断对错。Tell whether the following statements are true (T) or false (F).

   ① 检查导轨时，要检查导轨是否变形。　　　　　　（　　）
   ② 电梯各列导轨不能有台阶。　　　　　　　　　　（　　）
   ③ 要观察导轨表面是否有凹坑。　　　　　　　　　（　　）
   ④ 要检查导轨连接板上的螺栓。　　　　　　　　　（　　）

2. 选词填空。Choose the words to fill in the blanks.

   ① 检查导轨从（　　　）进入轿顶。　　　　A. 层站　　B. 顶层
   ② 检查各列导轨是否有（　　　）。　　　　A. 台阶　　B. 松动
   ③ 导轨表面不能有（　　　）和锈蚀。　　　A. 凹坑　　B. 灰尘
   ④ 用（　　　）检查导轨连接板的螺栓是否松动。　A. 万用表　B. 扳手

学习语法 Grammar

 语法点 1 Grammar Point 1

介词"从" The Preposition "从"

"从" indicates the start of an action. A sentence usually goes like "从 + Noun + Phrasal Verb". For example,

例句	英文翻译
Cóng dǐngcéng jìnrù jiāodǐng. 从 顶层 进入 轿顶。	Step on the elevator car roof from the top floor.
Cóng céngzhàn wài dǎkāi céngmén. 从 层站 外打开 层门。	Open the landing door from outside the leveling area.

(续表)

例句	英文翻译
Cóng chūyóukǒu fàng chulai rùnhuáyóu. 从 出油口 放 出来 润滑油。	Drain the lubricant from the oil outlet.

选词填空。 Choose the words to fill in the blanks.

1. （　　）层站打开轿门。　　　　　　A. 从　　B. 向
2. （　　）机房检查曳引机。　　　　　A. 从　　B. 在
3. （　　）最上方开始检查导轨。　　　A. 从　　B. 向
4. 电梯工（　　）轿顶工作。　　　　　A. 从　　B. 在

语法点 2　Grammar Point 2

介词"对于"　The Preposition "对于"

"对于" is a preposition which indicates the object of an action. A sentence usually goes like "对于 + Noun, … (an action)". For example,

例句	英文翻译
Duìyú dǎoguǐ, mùcè shìfǒu biànxíng. 对于导轨，目测是否变形。	Check if the guide rails are deformed.
Duìyú dǎoguǐ biǎomiàn, mùcè shìfǒu yǒu āokēng hé xiùshí. 对于导轨 表面，目测是否有凹坑和锈蚀。	Check if there are dents and corrosion on the rails' surface
Duìyú dǎoguǐ liánjiēbǎn shang de luóshuān, yòng bānshou jiǎnchá shìfǒu sōngdòng. 对于导轨连接板 上 的 螺栓，用 扳手检查是否 松动。	Check with a wrench if the bolts on the rail gussets have become loose.

第 19 课 ｜ 检查导轨

连词成句。 **Rearrange the words into sentences.**

1. ①导轨　②目测　③先　④对于　⑤变形　⑥是否
   → _____

2. ①螺栓　②扳手　③检查　④对于　⑤用　⑥要
   → _____

3. ①万用表　②对于　③要　④是否　⑤检查　⑥正常
   → _____

4. ①对于　②导轨表面　③凹坑　④检查　⑤是否　⑥有
   → _____

汉字书写 Writing Chinese Characters

chē 车 车 车 车
车 车 车 车 车

guǐ 轨 轨 轨 轨 轨 轨
轨 轨 轨 轨 轨

lún 轮 轮 轮 轮 轮 轮 轮
轮 轮 轮 轮 轮

zhóu 轴 轴 轴 轴 轴 轴 轴 轴
轴 轴 轴 轴 轴

# 职业拓展 Career Insight

群控电梯 Group-Controlled Elevators

A group-controlled elevator system refers to multiple elevators that share call buttons in the lobby and are automatically scheduled and assigned by a centralized control system. The system is especially suited for high-rise buildings, serving for boosting load efficiency and ride access.
There are multiple operating modes for the elevators, based on the time of the day and traffic needs (e.g., the peak mode and off-peak mode). Fuzzy algorithms can also be used to assign the optimal elevator to each call. The Destination Oriented Allocation System (DOAS) is another algorithm that allows passengers to input their destination floors before entering the elevator. It can minimize elevator car operations and landing instances for enhanced ride safety and comfort.

# 小结 Summary

 词语 Words

朗读下列词语。Read aloud the following words.

从	变形	台阶	高度
列	凹坑	锈蚀	螺栓
扳手	松动		

第 19 课 | 检查导轨

语法 Grammar

朗读下列句子。Read aloud the following sentences.

1. 从顶层进入轿顶。
2. 从层站外打开层门。
3. 对于导轨表面,目测是否有凹坑和锈蚀。
4. 对于导轨连接板上的螺栓,用扳手检查是否松动。

课文理解 Text Comprehension

复述课文内容。Retell the text.

1. 从顶层……,检修……,目测……。
2. 检查各列导轨……,台阶高度……。
3. 查看导轨表面……和锈蚀。
4. 对于……,用扳手……。

第 20 课 Lesson 20

Jiǎnchá gāngsīshéng
检查钢丝绳
Inspect the Steel Wire Rope

 **复习 Revision**

根据上一课课文选图填空。Choose the pictures to fill in the blanks based on the previous text.

　　　　　　　　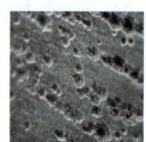

A.　　　　　　　　　B.　　　　　　　　　C.

查看导轨表面是否有_____和_____。

 **热身 Warm-up**

看图连线。Look at the pictures and match them with the words.

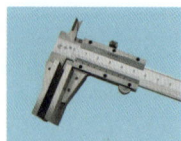　　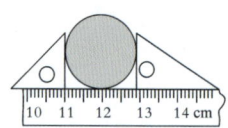　　　　　　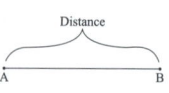

chuízhí	kuānqiánkǒu	yóubiāo kǎchǐ	xiāngjù	zhíjìng	gāngsīshéng
垂直	宽钳口	游标卡尺	相距	直径	钢丝绳
perpendicular	wide pliers	vernier caliper	at a distance of	diameter	steel wire rope

178

第 20 课 ｜ 检查钢丝绳

 学习生词 Words and Expressions 20-01

1	钢丝绳	gāngsīshéng	n.	steel wire rope
2	相距	xiāngjù	v.	be apart
3	米	mǐ	m.	meter
4	点	diǎn	n.	point
5	宽钳口游标卡尺	kuānqiánkǒu yóubiāo kǎchǐ	phr.	wide-mouth vernier caliper
6	直径	zhíjìng	n.	diameter
7	每	měi	pron.	each, every
8	互相	hùxiāng	adv.	mutually
9	垂直	chuízhí	v.	(be) perpendicular
10	方向	fāngxiàng	n.	direction
11	次	cì	m.	time
12	平均值	píngjūnzhí	n.	average (value)
13	如果	rúguǒ	conj.	if
14	公称直径	gōngchēng zhíjìng	phr.	nominal diameter
15	必须	bìxū	adv.	must

词语练习 Word Exercises

1. 认读词语。Recognize and read the words.

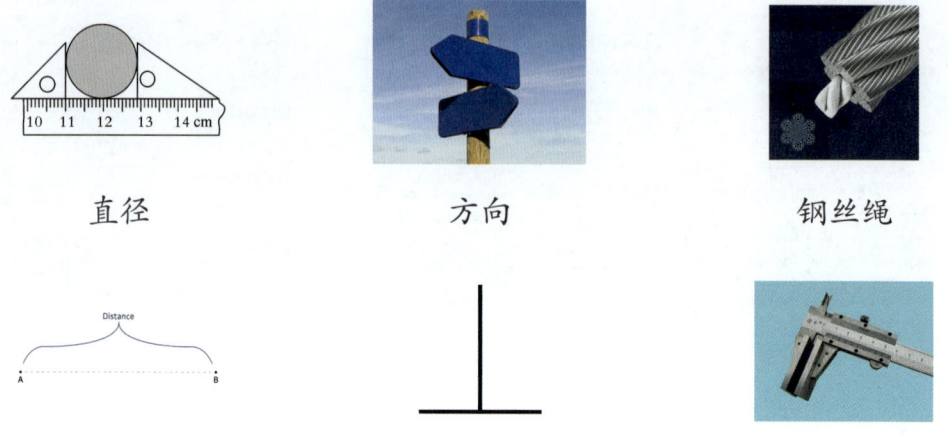

直径　　　　　　方向　　　　　　钢丝绳

相距　　　　　　垂直　　　　　　宽钳口游标卡尺

2. 朗读词语搭配。Read aloud the word collocations.

❶ 方向	垂直方向
	运行方向
❷ 互相	互相垂直
	互相帮助（bāngzhù, help）
❸ 直径	公称直径
	测量直径
❹ 检查	检查钢丝绳
	检查游标卡尺

第20课 | 检查钢丝绳

 学习课文 Text 🎧 20-02

检查 钢丝绳
Jiǎnchá gāngsīshéng

进入轿顶,在钢丝绳上选择相距一米的两个点。用宽钳口游标卡尺测量直径,在每点互相垂直方向上测量两次,四次的平均值就是钢丝绳的直径。如果钢丝绳直径小于公称直径的90%[①],必须更换钢丝绳。

Inspect the Steel Wire Rope

Enter the elevator car roof, and pick two points one meter apart on the steel wire rope. Measure the diameter of the wire rope—measure it twice, in mutually perpendicular directions, at each point with a wide-mouth vernier caliper. The average of the four readings is the diameter of the rope. The steel wire rope must be replaced if the measured value is less than 90% of the nominal diameter.

---

① 90% 读作"百分之九十"(bǎi fēn zhī jiǔshí)。

课文练习 Text Exercises

1. 判断对错。Tell whether the following statements are true (T) or false (F).

   ① 要在轿顶检查钢丝绳。   (   )
   ② 测量直径的工具是宽钳口游标卡尺。   (   )
   ③ 在钢丝绳上选择两个点，每个点测量四次直径。   (   )
   ④ 钢丝绳直径不能小于公称直径的 90%。   (   )

2. 选词填空。Choose the words to fill in the blanks.

   ① 在钢丝绳上（   ）相距一米的两个点。
      A. 查看   B. 选择   C. 观察
   ② 在每点（   ）垂直方向上测量两次。
      A. 互相   B. 目测   C. 完全
   ③ （   ）测量的平均值就是钢丝绳的直径。
      A. 两次   B. 一次   C. 四次
   ④ 钢丝绳直径（   ）公称直径的 90%，必须更换钢丝绳。
      A. 大于   B. 小于

 学习语法 Grammar

语法点 1 Grammar Point 1

动量词"次" The Verbal Measure Word "次"

"次" is a measure word to indicate how often an action happens. A sentence usually goes like "Verb + Number + 次 (+ object)". For example,

第 20 课 | 检查钢丝绳

例句	英文翻译
Sì cì cèliáng de píngjūnzhí jiù shì gāngsīshéng zhíjìng. 四次测量的平均值就是钢丝绳直径。	The average of the four readings is the diameter of the steel wire rope.
Měi shíwǔ tiān jìnxíng yí cì diàntī wéibǎo. 每十五天进行一次电梯维保。	The elevator is maintained every 15 days.
Zhège diàntī sānshí tiān li fāshēngle sì cì gùzhàng. 这个电梯三十天里发生了四次故障。	This elevator has broken down four times in 30 days.

选词填空。Choose the words to fill in the blanks.

1. 钢丝绳直径要进行四（　　）测量。　A. 次　　B. 个　　C. 把
2. 轿厢里面有四（　　）乘客。　　　　A. 次　　B. 个　　C. 把
3. 钢丝绳直径要测量四（　　）。　　　A. 次　　B. 个　　C. 把
4. 轿顶里面有一（　　）游标卡尺。　　A. 次　　B. 个　　C. 把

 语法点 2 Grammar Point 2

副词"必须" The Adverb "必须"

"必须" is used before a verb to indicate that something is very necessary, either considering the facts or feelings. For example,

例句	英文翻译
Rúguǒ gāngsīshéng zhíjìng xiǎoyú gōngchēng zhíjìng de 90%, 如果钢丝绳直径小于公称直径的 90%， bìxū gēnghuàn gāngsīshéng. 必须更换钢丝绳。	The steel wire rope must be replaced if its diameter is less than 90% of the nominal diameter.
Diàntī jǐngdào lǐmiàn bìxū yǒu zhàomíngdēng. 电梯井道里面必须有照明灯。	Lights are necessary in the hoistway of the elevator.
Diàntīgōng bìxū zhùyì ānquán. 电梯工必须注意安全。	Elevator workers must stay safe.

183

连词成句。Rearrange the words into sentences.

1. ①安全　②注意　③工作　④要　⑤时　⑥必须
   → _____

2. ①工作　②穿　③时　④绝缘鞋　⑤要　⑥必须
   → _____

3. ①万用表　②必须　③是否　④正常　⑤检查
   → _____

4. ①打开　②层门　③三角钥匙　④必须　⑤使用
   → _____

 汉字书写 Writing Chinese Characters

第 20 课 | 检查钢丝绳

文化拓展 Culture Insight

中国空间站 China's Space Station

Initiated in 1992, China's Space Station project endeavors to establish an enduring human-occupied and autonomously operating space laboratory. Weighing close to 100 tons, the station consists of four parts and can house three astronauts as long-term residents. It actually has a maximum load capacity of six astronauts. By July 2024, China's Space Station has carried out more than 130 scientific research and application projects in orbit. In addition to its role as China's space laboratory, China's Space Station acts as a platform facilitating joint efforts with international partners. Widened collaborations will be in sight between China and the UN and other countries (and other international organizations as well) for the common interests of human beings in the outer space.

小结 Summary

词语 Words

朗读下列词语。Read aloud the following words.

米	宽钳口游标卡尺	钢丝绳
次	如果	直径
垂直	必须	

185

语法 Grammar

朗读下列句子。Read aloud the following sentences.

1. 在每点相互垂直方向上测量两次。
2. 四次测量的平均值就是钢丝绳的直径。
3. 如果钢丝绳直径小于公称直径的 90%，必须更换钢丝绳。
4. 电梯工必须注意安全。

课文理解 Text Comprehension

复述课文内容。Retell the text.

1. 进入……，在……的两个点。
2. 用宽钳口……，在每点……两次，……就是钢丝绳的直径。
3. 如果钢丝绳直径……，必须……。

第 21 课　进入轿顶
Lesson 21　Enter the Elevator Car Roof

 复习 Revision

根据图片选择词语。Choose the words based on the pictures.

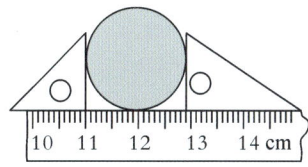

1　直径（　　）
　　测量（　　）

2　钢丝绳（　　）
　　补偿链（　　）

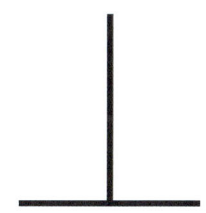

3　垂直（　　）
　　互相（　　）

4　游标卡尺（　　）
　　宽钳口游标卡尺（　　）

热身 Warm-up

看图选词，将对应的字母填在括号里。Look at the pictures and choose the words. Put the corresponding letters in the brackets.

A. 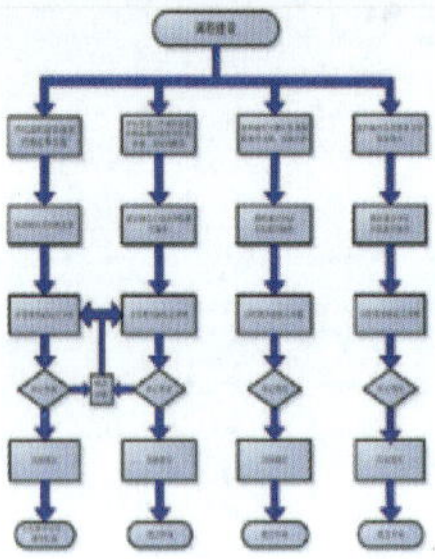　　　　　　　　　B. 　　　　　　　　　C.

D. 　　　　　　　　　E. 　　　　　　　　　F.

1	门锁	ménsuǒ	door lock	(　　)
2	风险	fēngxiǎn	risk	(　　)
3	门缝	ménfèng	door gap	(　　)
4	规范	guīfàn	standardized	(　　)
5	呼叫	hūjiào	call	(　　)
6	流程	liúchéng	procedure	(　　)

第 21 课 | 进入轿顶

学习生词 Words and Expressions 🎧 21-01

1	风险	fēngxiǎn	n.	risk
2	遵守	zūnshǒu	v.	follow, observe
3	规范	guīfàn	adj./n.	standardized; standard
4	流程	liúchéng	n.	procedure
5	防止	fángzhǐ	v.	prevent
6	呼叫	hūjiào	v.	call
7	合适	héshì	adj.	appropriate
8	扒	bā	v.	*force something open (by hands)*
9	条	tiáo	m.	*a measure word for long, thin objects*
10	门缝	ménfèng	n.	door gap
11	验证	yànzhèng	v.	verify
12	门锁	ménsuǒ	n.	door lock

词语练习 Word Exercises

1. 认读词语。Recognize and read the words.

风险

规范

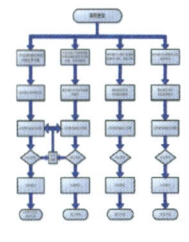
流程

| | 呼叫 | 门锁 | 门缝 |

2. 朗读词语搭配。Read aloud the word collocations.

❶ 验证	验证门锁	
	验证急停开关	
❷ 扒	扒开层门	
❸ 呼叫	呼叫电梯	

 学习课文 Text 🎧 21-02

进入 轿顶
Jìnrù jiàodǐng

Jìnrù jiàodǐng yǒu fēngxiǎn, yīnggāi zūnshǒu guīfàn liúchéng:
进入 轿顶 有 风险,应该 遵守 规范 流程:

Céngmén wàimiàn fàng hùlán, fángzhǐ chéngkè jìnrù;
1. 层门 外面 放 护栏,防止 乘客 进入;

第21课 | 进入轿顶

2. 呼叫电梯，电梯运行到合适的位置，插入并旋转三角钥匙；

3. 扒开一条门缝，然后放顶门器，按外呼按钮，验证门锁，此时电梯不能运行；

4. 打开层门，按下急停开关，关门后按按钮，验证急停开关，此时电梯不能运行；

5. 再打开层门，进入轿顶。

Enter the Elevator Car Roof

As entering the car roof carries risks, elevator workers should follow the standardized procedures:

1. Place the guard rail outside the landing door to prevent passengers from entering;

2. Insert the triangle key and rotate it after the elevator travels to an appropriate place by a call;

3. Force the door open, and then put a door stopper on the door gap. Press the call button to verify the door lock. The elevator won't move in this case;

4. Open the landing door and press the stop button. Press the call button to verify the stop button after the door is closed. The elevator won't move in this case;

5. Open the landing door again and enter the roof.

课文练习 Text Exercises

1. 判断对错。Tell whether the following statements are true (T) or false (F).

   ① 进入轿顶有风险。 ( )
   ② 进入轿顶前，层门外面要放护栏。 ( )
   ③ 进入轿顶前，要准备三角钥匙和顶门器。 ( )
   ④ 进入轿顶要验证门锁和急停开关是否正常。 ( )

2. 选词填空。Choose the words to fill in the blanks.

   ① 进入轿顶要遵守规范的（　　）。　　A. 流程　　B. 要求
   ② 按按钮是为了（　　）门锁和急停开关。　　A. 验证　　B. 检查
   ③ 验证急停开关要（　　）层门。　　A. 打开　　B. 关闭
   ④ 扒开（　　）门缝，再放入顶门器。　　A. 一条　　B. 一个

学习语法 Grammar

语法点1 Grammar Point 1

动词 + 到 + 地点　V + "到" + Location

"到" is a resultative complement. The structure indicates the completion of an action. For example,

例句	英文翻译
Hūjiào diàntī, diàntī yùnxíng dào héshì de wèizhì. 呼叫 电梯，电梯 运行 到 合适 的 位置。	The elevator travels to an appropriate place by a call.
Diàntī yùnxíng dào néng jìnrù jiàodǐng de wèizhì. 电梯 运行 到 能 进入 轿顶 的 位置。	The elevator travels to a place from which people can enter the car roof.

(续表)

例句	英文翻译
Diàntī yùnxíng dào néng jiǎnchá céngmén de wèizhì. 电梯 运行 到 能 检查 层门 的 位置。	The elevator travels to a place where the landing door can be inspected.

连词成句。Rearrange the words into sentences.

1. ①三角钥匙　②开　③用　④层门　⑤打
   → _____

2. ①电梯工　②扒　③一条　④开　⑤门缝　⑥了
   → _____

3. ①把　②合适的　③电梯　④运行　⑤到　⑥位置
   → _____

4. ①电梯　②检修状态　③转换　④到　⑤把
   → _____

语法点 2　Grammar Point 2

动词 + 开　V+ "开"

"开" is a resultative complement. A resultative complement is used after a verb to show the result of an action. It is usually used in the sentence structure: "Verb + Resultative Complement + Object". For example,

例句	英文翻译
Diàntīgōng dǎkāi céngmén. 电梯工 打开 层门。	The elevator worker opens the landing door.
Diàntīgōng bākāi ménfèng, fàng dǐngménqì. 电梯工 扒开 门缝，放 顶门器。	The elevator worker forces the door open and puts a door stopper.

(续表)

例句	英文翻译
Yòng sōngzhá bānshou sōngkāi zhìdòngqì. 用 松闸 扳手 松开 制动器。	Loosen the brake with a brake release wrench.

选词填空。Choose the words to fill in the blanks.

1. 电梯工进入机房，断（　　）电源。　　A. 开　　B. 上　　C. 到
2. 打（　　）减速箱，放出旧润滑油。　　A. 开　　B. 上　　C. 到
3. 关闭电源盒，挂（　　）标牌。　　　　A. 开　　B. 上　　C. 到
4. 把护栏放（　　）轿厢里面。　　　　　A. 开　　B. 上　　C. 到

 汉字书写 Writing Chinese Characters

nǚ 女 女 女
女 女 女 女 女

zǐ 子 子 子
子 子 子 子 子

hǎo 好 好 好 好 好 好
好 好 好 好 好

mā 妈 妈 妈 妈 妈 妈
妈 妈 妈 妈 妈

职业拓展 Career Insight

螺旋型自动扶梯 Spiral Escalator

In 1985, Mitsubishi Electric installed the world's first spiral escalator at Umeda subway station in Osaka, Japan. The hallmark of such an escalator lies in its capability to shift between horizontal and vertical dimensions, fashioning a graceful arc that delivers a unique experience to those who ride it. These escalators are not merely space-saving  devices. The artistic features also make them an architectual ornament that infuses the city with an eye-catching landscape.

小结 Summary

 词语 Words

朗读下列词语。Read aloud the following words.

| 风险 | 规范 | 流程 | 验证 |
| 条 | 遵守 | 呼叫 | 扒开 |

语法 Grammar

朗读下列句子。Read aloud the following sentences.

1. 呼叫电梯，电梯运行到合适的位置。
2. 电梯运行到能检查层门的位置。
3. 电梯工扒开门缝，放顶门器。
4. 打开层门，按下急停开关。

课文理解 Text Comprehension

复述课文内容。Retell the text.

1. 进入轿顶……，应该……。
2. ……，防止……；
3. 呼叫……，运行……，插入……；
4. 扒开……，然后放……，按……，验证……，此时……；
5. 打开……，按下……，关门……，验证……，此时……；
6. 再打开……，进入……。

第 22 课
Lesson 22

Yànzhèng jiǎnxiū zhuàngtài
验证检修状态
Verify the Inspection Mode

 复习 Revision

根据图片选择词语。Choose the words based on the pictures.

1. 风险（　　）
   流程（　　）

2. 遵守（　　）
   门锁（　　）

3. 门缝（　　）
   层门（　　）

4. 呼叫（　　）
   遵守（　　）

热身 Warm-up

看图选词，把对应的字母填在括号里。Look at the pictures and choose the words. Put the corresponding letters in the brackets.

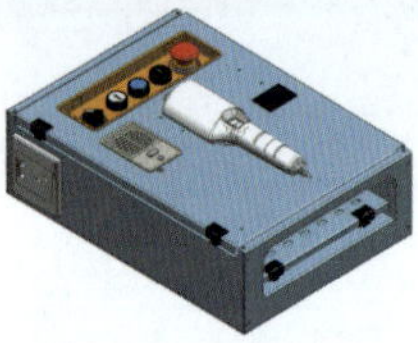

A. 　　　　　　　　B. 　　　　　　　　C.

D.　　　　　　　　E. 　　　　　　　　F.

1	黄色	huángsè	yellow	(　　)
2	不要倚靠	búyào yǐkào	No Leaning	(　　)
3	公共按钮	gōnggòng ànniǔ	public button	(　　)
4	栏杆	lángān	parapet	(　　)
5	检修箱	jiǎnxiūxiāng	inspection box	(　　)
6	反绳轮	fǎnshénglún	suspension sheave	(　　)

第 22 课 | 验证检修状态

 学习生词 Words and Expressions 22-01

1	外	wài	n.	outside
2	检修箱	jiǎnxiūxiāng	n.	inspection box
3	拍	pāi	v.	tap
4	接着	jiēzhe	adv.	then, later
5	复位	fù//wèi	v.	reset
6	检修	jiǎnxiū	v.	inspect
7	公共按钮	gōnggòng ànniǔ		public button
8	不要	búyào	adv.	(do) not
9	倚靠	yǐkào	v.	lean
10	黄色	huángsè	n.	yellow
11	栏杆	lángān	n.	parapet
12	触碰	chùpèng	v.	touch
13	反绳轮	fǎnshénglún	n.	suspension sheave

词语练习 Word Exercises

1. 认读词语。Recognize and read the words.

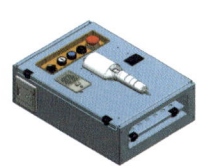

检修箱

公共按钮

反绳轮

不要倚靠　　　　　　黄色　　　　　　　栏杆

2. 朗读词语搭配。Read aloud the word collocations.

❶ 黄色	黄色按钮	
	黄色安全帽	
❷ 栏杆	轿顶栏杆	
	黄色栏杆	
❸ 反绳轮	轿顶反绳轮	
❹ 触碰	触碰极限开关	

第 22 课 | 验证检修状态

 学习课文 Text 🎧 22-02

验证 检修 状态
Yànzhèng jiǎnxiū zhuàngtài

从层站外打开层门，在检修箱上拍下急停开关，旋转检修开关到检修状态。接着，进入轿顶，复位急停开关。按下检修公共按钮和上下行按钮，测试电梯能否运行。在轿顶时，不要倚靠黄色栏杆，不要触碰反绳轮等部件。

Verify the Inspection Mode

Open the landing door from outside the landing, tap the stop button on the inspection box, and rotate the switch to the "Inspection" mode. Then, enter the car roof to reset the stop button. Press the public controls and buttons "Up" and "Down" to test if the elevator can move. Do not lean on the yellow parapets or touch the suspension sheave and other parts on the car roof.

课文练习 Text Exercises

1. 判断对错。Tell whether the following statements are true (T) or false (F).

   ① 上轿顶时,要从层站外打开层门。 （　　）
   ② 急停开关在检修箱上。 （　　）
   ③ 验证检修状态,要进入轿顶。 （　　）
   ④ 在轿顶时,可以触碰反绳轮等部件。 （　　）

2. 选词填空。Choose the words to fill in the blanks.

   ① 先拍下急停开关,再进入（　　）。　A. 轿顶　　B. 层站
   ② 为了安全,在轿顶,不能倚靠（　　）。　A. 栏杆　　B. 护栏
   ③ 按下按钮是为了验证（　　）。　A. 检修状态　B. 正常运行
   ④ 检修箱上有（　　）。　A. 栏杆　　B. 公共按钮

学习语法 Grammar

语法点 1 Grammar Point 1

动词 + 下　V + "下"

"下" is used after a verb to indicate a downward action. For example,

例句	英文翻译
Zài jiǎnxiūxiāng shang pāixia jítíng kāiguān. 在 检修箱 上 拍下 急停 开关。	Tap the stop button on the inspection box.
Zài jiāodǐng ànxia gōnggòng ànniǔ. 在 轿顶 按下 公共 按钮。	Press the common button on the car roof.
Zài céngmén ànxia céngzhàn ànniǔ. 在 层站 按下 层站 按钮。	Press the landing button on the landing.

第 22 课 | 验证检修状态

选词填空。Choose the words to fill in the blanks.

1. 电梯工进入机房,断(　　)电源。　　A. 开　　B. 上　　C. 下
2. 电梯工进入轿顶,拍(　　)急停开关。　A. 开　　B. 上　　C. 下
3. 关闭电源盒,挂(　　)标牌。　　　　A. 开　　B. 上　　C. 下
4. 在顶层,按(　　)层站按钮。　　　　A. 开　　B. 上　　C. 下

语法点 2 Grammar Point 2

副词"接着" The Adverb "接着"

"接着" means that one thing happens after another immediately. For example,

例句	英文翻译
Dǎkāi céngmén, jiēzhe pāixia jítíng kāiguān. 打开 层门,接着拍下 急停 开关。	Open the landing door and (then) press the stop button.
Jìnrù jiàoxiāng, jiēzhe xuǎnzé lóucéng. 进入 轿厢,接着 选择 楼层。	Enter the elevator car and (then) select the floor.
Chuānshang gōngzuòfú, jiēzhe dàishang ānquánmào. 穿上 工作服,接着 戴上 安全帽。	Put on the work clothes and (then) the safety helmet.

改写句子。Rewrite the sentences.

1. 进入轿顶后,打开照明。
   ＿＿＿＿＿＿＿＿＿＿接着＿＿＿＿＿＿＿＿＿＿＿。

2. 先断开电源,再打开减速箱。
   ＿＿＿＿＿＿＿＿＿＿接着＿＿＿＿＿＿＿＿＿＿＿。

3. 先扒开一条门缝,再放顶门器。
   ＿＿＿＿＿＿＿＿＿＿接着＿＿＿＿＿＿＿＿＿＿＿。

4. 打开层门后,按急停开关。
   ＿＿＿＿＿＿＿＿＿＿接着＿＿＿＿＿＿＿＿＿＿＿。

汉字书写 Writing Chinese Characters

lì 立
chǎn 产
xīn 辛
wèi 位

文化拓展 Culture Insight

共享单车 Shared Bikes

Taking a shared bike is a new way of traveling that uses Internet technology for bike rental and return. Being a convenient, low-carbon, and green mobility option, it also helps ease traffic congestion and reduce air pollution in urban areas. The feature of shared bikes is their dockless system, allowing users to pick up and park bikes anywhere at any time, thereby saving time in finding and securing

parking spots. Users can unlock or lock a bicycle via QR codes scanning or NFC with their mobile phones. They can use shared bikes for a short-distance travel, or ride them to subway stations or bus stops for transfers. The bike-sharing system, as a supplementary mode to public transport, makes it easier and quicker to get around cities, helps people stay healthy and eco-friendly, and contributes to an overall better urban lifestyle.

小结 Summary

词语 Words

朗读下列词语。Read aloud the following words.

| 检修箱 | 不要 | 复位 | 接着 |
| 倚靠 | 黄色 | 栏杆 | 反绳轮 |

语法 Grammar

朗读下列句子。Read aloud the following sentences.

1. 在检修箱上拍下急停开关。
2. 在轿顶按下公共按钮。
3. 进入轿厢，接着选择楼层。
4. 打开层门，接着按下急停开关。

课文理解 Text Comprehension

复述课文内容。Retell the text.

1. 从层站外……，在……，旋转……。
2. 接着，进入……，复位……。
3. 按下……和……，测试……。
4. 在轿顶时，……，……等部件。

第 23 课 Lesson 23

Jiǎnchá duìzhòng 检查对重
Inspect the Counterweight

 ### 复习 Revision

根据图片，在括号里填入对应的字母。Fill in the corresponding letters in the brackets according to the pictures.

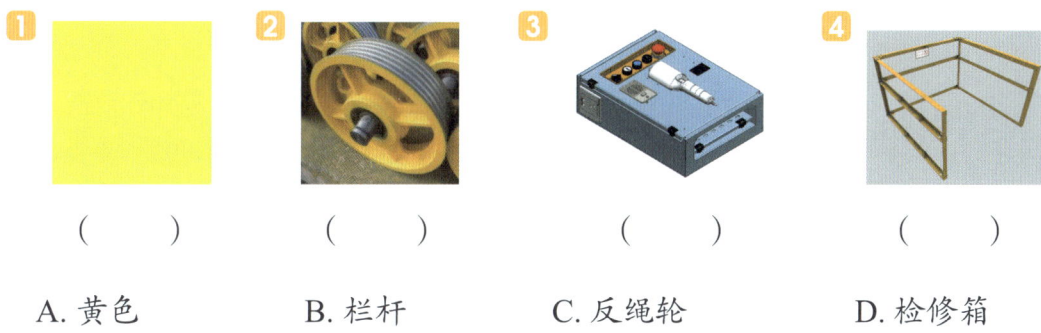

A. 黄色　　　B. 栏杆　　　C. 反绳轮　　　D. 检修箱

 ### 热身 Warm-up

看图选词，把对应的字母填在括号里。Look at the pictures and choose the words. Put the corresponding letters in the brackets.

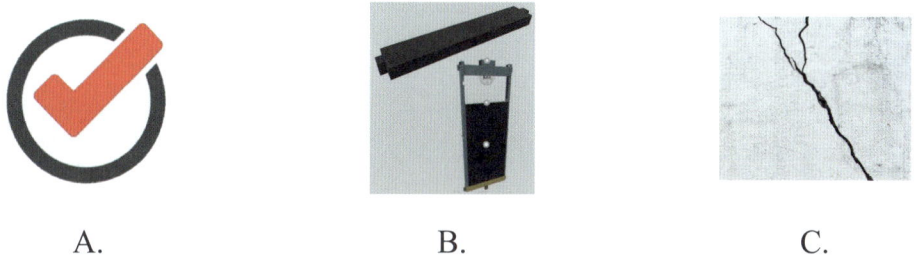

A.　　　　　　B.　　　　　　C.

207

D.　　　　　　　　　　　E.　　　　　　　　　　　F.

1	压板	yābǎn	pressure plate	( )
2	正确	zhèngquè	correct	( )
3	开裂	kāiliè	crack	( )
4	边缘	biānyuán	edge	( )
5	破碎	pòsuì	break	( )
6	对重块	duìzhòngkuài	counterweight filler	( )

 学习生词 Words and Expressions  23-01

1	让	ràng	v.	allow, let
2	对重块	duìzhòngkuài	n.	counterweight filler
3	数量	shùliàng	n.	quantity
4	标识	biāoshí	n.	mark
5	清晰	qīngxī	adj.	clear
6	正确	zhèngquè	adj.	correct
7	开裂	kāiliè	v.	crack
8	破碎	pòsuì	v.	break

9	现象	xiànxiàng	n.	phenomenon
10	压板	yābǎn	n.	pressure plate
11	也	yě	adv.	also (in a positive statement), nor (in a negative statement)
12	移位	yí//wèi	v.	displace
13	边缘	biānyuán	n.	edge

词语练习 Word Exercises

1. 认读词语。Recognize and read the words.

正确

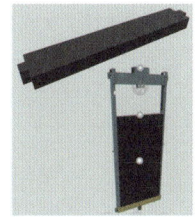
对重块

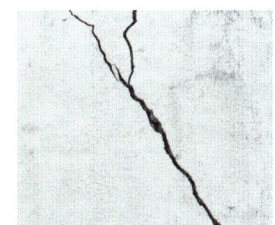
开裂

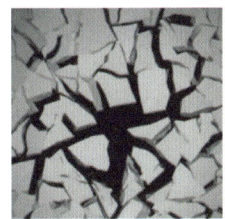
破碎

压板

边缘

2. 朗读词语搭配。Read aloud the word collocations.

❶ 数量标识		
❷ 开裂	墙壁（qiángbì, wall）开裂	
❸ 破碎	玻璃（bōli, glass）破碎	
❹ 边缘	轿顶边缘	

学习课文 Text 🎧 23-02

Jiǎnchá duìzhòng
检查 对重

Jìnrù jiǎodǐng hòu, ràng jiāoxiāng yùnxíng dào shǒu néng pèngdào
进入轿顶后，让轿厢运行到手能碰到

duìzhòng de wèizhì. Xiān mùcè duìzhòngkuài shang de shùliàng biāoshí
对重的位置。先目测对重块上的数量标识

shìfǒu qīngxī zhèngquè, guānchá duìzhòngkuài shìfǒu yǒu kāiliè、
是否清晰正确，观察对重块是否有开裂、

第 23 课 | 检查对重

pòsuì děng xiànxiàng; zài jiǎnchá duìzhòng yābǎn, quèbǎo duìzhòngkuài
破碎 等 现象；再 检查 对重 压板，确保 对重块
méiyǒu sōngdòng, yě méiyǒu yíwèi; zuìhòu cèliáng duìzhòng hé
没有 松动，也 没有 移位；最后 测量 对重 和
jiàoxiāng biānyuán de jùlí.
轿厢 边缘 的 距离。

Inspect the Counterweight

After entering the elevator car roof, drive the car to a place where one can reach the counterweight. See if the quantity marks on the counterweight filler are clear and accurate, and then check for problems such as cracking or breaking. Check the counterweight pressure plates and make sure that the filler is neither loose nor displaced. Finally, measure the distance between the counterweight and the edge of the car.

课文练习 Text Exercises

1. 判断对错。Tell whether the following statements are true (T) or false (F).

   ① 检查对重要在轿顶进行。　　　　　　　　　　　　　（　　）
   ② 对重上必须有数量标识。　　　　　　　　　　　　　（　　）
   ③ 对重不能有开裂和破碎等现象。　　　　　　　　　　（　　）
   ④ 对重块松动和移位都是不符合要求的。　　　　　　　（　　）

2. 选词填空。Choose the words to fill in the blanks.

   ① 让轿厢运行到手能碰到（　　）的位置。　A. 极限开关　B. 对重
   ② （　　）对重块上的数量标识是否清晰正确。　A. 目测　　B. 检查

③ 测量对重和（　　）边缘的距离。　　A. 轿厢　　B. 护栏
④ 检查（　　），确保对重块无松动。　　A. 压板　　B. 螺栓

学习语法 Grammar

语法点1 Grammar Point 1

动词"让" The Verb "让"

The verb "让" means making somebody/something to produce a certain result. A sentence usually goes like "Subject + 让 + Object + Verb + Other Element". For example,

例句	英文翻译
Ràng jiàoxiāng yùnxíng dào shǒu néng pèngdào duìzhòng de wèizhì. 让 轿厢 运行 到 手 能 碰到 对重 的 位置。	Drive the elevator car to a place where one can reach the counterweight.
Ràng diàntīgōng dàishang ānquánmào. 让 电梯工 戴上 安全帽。	Let the elevator worker wear a safety helmet.
Ràng diàntīgōng ānquán jìnrù jiàodǐng. 让 电梯工 安全 进入 轿顶。	Let the elevator worker step on the car roof safely.

连词成句。Rearrange the words into sentences.

❶ ①电梯 ②转换 ③让 ④到 ⑤检修状态 → _____
❷ ①乘客 ②快速 ③轿厢 ④让 ⑤进入 → _____
❸ ①让 ②合适的 ③电梯 ④运行 ⑤到 ⑥位置 → _____
❹ ①电梯工 ②工作服 ③穿上 ④让 → _____

语法点 2 Grammar Point 2

副词"也" The Adverb "也"

"也" is used before a verb to indicate being or doing the same as others or to show two equally important things. For example,

例句	英文翻译
Quèbǎo duìzhòng wú sōngdòng, yě méiyǒu yíwèi. 确保 对重 无 松动，也没有 移位。	Make sure the counterweight is neither loose nor displaced.
Diànyuánhé yào guàshang biāopái, yě yào guàshang suǒ. 电源盒 要 挂上 标牌，也要 挂上 锁。	The power box should be labeled and (also) locked.
Duìzhòng yào jiǎnchá shùliàng biāoshí, yě yào jiǎnchá shìfǒu kāiliè. 对重 要 检查 数量 标识，也要 检查 是否 开裂。	For the counterweight, it is necessary to check the quantity marks and whether it has a cracking.

选词填空。Choose the words to fill in the blanks.

1. 在机房，要检查曳引机，（　　）要检查控制柜。　　A. 也　　B. 都
2. 进入轿顶，要戴安全帽，（　　）要穿绝缘鞋。　　A. 也　　B. 都
3. 老师和学生（　　）在轿顶。　　A. 也　　B. 都
4. 曳引轮的声音很大和曳引机振动，（　　）说明有故障。
　　　　　　　　　　　　　　　　　　　　A. 也　　B. 都

汉字书写 Writing Chinese Characters

wén
文 文 文 文

文 文 文 文 文

 **职业拓展** Career Insight

全球最快的电梯之一——广州周大福金融中心超高速电梯
The Elevator at Chow Tai Fook Finance Centre in Guangzhou—One of the Fastest Elevators in the World

The Chow Tai Fook Finance Center is a supertall complex in the Pearl River New Town, Guangzhou. The giant of 530 meters high is a masterpiece of KPF. One of the 86 Hitachi elevators it houses can travel 1,260 meters per minute, a Guinness record as the fastest elevator in the world. This elevator can whisk passengers from the ground level to  the hotel lobby on the 95th floor, which is 440 meters high, in approximately 42 seconds, akin to having a vertical subway system within the skyscraper.

小结 Summary

词语 Words

朗读下列词语。Read aloud the following words.

正确	对重块	开裂	破碎
压板	让	边缘	也

语法 Grammar

朗读下列句子。Read aloud the following sentences.

1. 让轿厢运行到手能碰到对重的位置。
2. 让电梯工戴上安全帽。
3. 对重块没有松动也没有移位。
4. 电源盒要挂上标牌，也要挂上锁。

课文理解 Text Comprehension

复述课文内容。Retell the text.

1. 进入……，让轿厢……位置。
2. 先目测……，观察……、……等现象；
3. 再检查……，确保……，也……；
4. 最后测量……的距离。

第24课 Lesson 24

检查油杯
Jiǎnchá yóubēi
Inspect the Oil Cup

 复习 Revision

根据图片选择词语。Choose the words based on the pictures.

1. 对重（　　）
   对重块（　　）

2. 压板（　　）
   松动（　　）

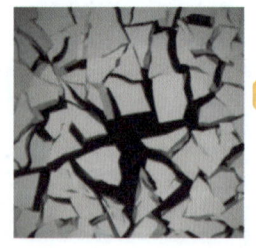

3. 破碎（　　）
   移位（　　）

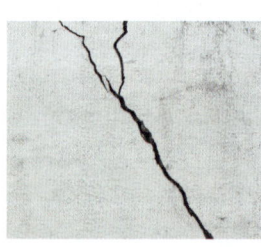

4. 开裂（　　）
   目测（　　）

第 24 课 | 检查油杯

 **热身 Warm-up**

看图连线。Look at the pictures and match them with the words.

yóuwèi	máozhān	dǐngbù	yóubēi
油位	毛毡	顶部	油杯
oil level	felt	top	oil cup

 **学习生词 Words and Expressions** 🎧 24-01

1	油杯	yóubēi	*n.*	oil cup
2	四	sì	*num.*	four
3	个	gè	*m.*	*a measure word for general use*
4	步骤	bùzhòu	*n.*	step
5	顶部	dǐngbù	*n.*	top
6	摇动	yáodòng	*v.*	shake
7	毛毡	máozhān	*n.*	felt
8	吸附	xīfù	*v.*	absorb
9	油位	yóuwèi	*n.*	oil level
10	大约	dàyuē	*adv.*	about

11	方法	fāngfǎ	n.	method
12	问题	wèntí	n.	problem
13	处理	chǔlǐ	v.	handle, deal with, address

词语练习 Word Exercises

1. 认读词语。Recognize and read the words.

　　　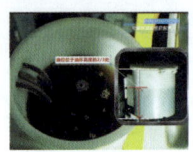　　　　　　

　　油杯　　　　　　油位　　　　　　毛毡　　　　　　顶部

2. 选择搭配。Choose and match.

①吸附（　　）　　②摇动（　　）　　③处理（　　）　　④查看（　　）

A. 油杯　　　　B. 问题　　　　C. 润滑油　　　　D. 毛毡

 学习课文 Text 🎧 24-02

检查 油杯 (Jiǎnchá yóubēi)

Jiǎnchá yóubēi yǒu sì gè bùzhòu:
检查 油杯 有 四 个 步骤：

Zài jiàoxiāng dǐngbù yáodòng yóubēi, jiǎnchá shìfǒu sōngdòng;
1. 在 轿厢 顶部 摇动 油杯，检查 是否 松动；

Chákàn máozhān shìfǒu xīfù rùnhuáyóu;
2. 查看 毛毡 是否 吸附 润滑油；

第24课 | 检查油杯

Xiàng yóubēi zhōng zhùrù rùnhuáyóu, yóuwèi dàyuē zài yóubēi gāodù 2/3 de wèizhì;
3. 向油杯中注入润滑油,油位大约在油杯高度2/3①的位置;

Yòng xiāngtóng de fāngfǎ jiǎnchá duìzhòng yóubēi. Rúguǒ yǒu wèntí, zé jìnxíng chǔlǐ.
4. 用相同的方法检查对重油杯。如果有问题,则进行处理。

Inspect the Oil Cup

Inspecting the oil cup consists of four steps:

1. Shake the oil cup at the top of the elevator car to check if the cup is loose;

2. Check if the felt absorbs the lubricant;

3. Fill the cup with lubricant to about 2/3 of the full mark;

4. Use the same method to check the counterweight's oil cup.

Remember to address problems, if any.

课文练习 Text Exercises

1. 判断对错。 Tell whether the following statements are true (T) or false (F).

1. 摇动油杯是为了检查是否松动。　　　　　　　　　　　（　　）
2. 毛毡需要吸附润滑油。　　　　　　　　　　　　　　　（　　）
3. 油杯里润滑油的高度是油位。　　　　　　　　　　　　（　　）
4. 对重油杯也需要检查。　　　　　　　　　　　　　　　（　　）

---

① 2/3 读作"三分之二"(sān fēn zhī èr)。

2. 选词填空。Choose the words to fill in the blanks.

1️⃣ 查看（　　）是否吸附润滑油。
　A. 毛毡　　　　B. 钢丝绳　　　　C. 油杯

2️⃣ 在轿厢顶部摇动油杯，检查是否（　　）。
　A. 松动　　　　B. 固定　　　　C. 正确

3️⃣ 向油杯中（　　）润滑油。
　A. 注入　　　　B. 进入　　　　C. 放

4️⃣ 对重油杯和轿厢油杯检查方法（　　）。
　A. 相同　　　　B. 垂直　　　　C. 遵守

学习语法 Grammar

语法点 1 Grammar Point 1

副词"大约" The Adverb "大约"

"大约" is used as an adverb before a number to indicate that the number is not precise. For example,

例句	英文翻译
Yóuwèi dàyuē zài yóubēi gāodù 2/3 de wèizhì. 油位大约在油杯高度 2/3 的位置。	The oil level stays at about 2/3 of the height of the oil cup.
Diàntī lǐmiàn dàyuē yǒu 30 gè chéngkè. 电梯里面大约有 30 个乘客。	There are about 30 passengers in the elevator.
Zhìdòngqì jiànxì dàyuē yǒu 0.7 háomǐ. 制动器间隙大约有 0.7 毫米。	The clearance of the brake is about 0.7 mm.

连词成句。Rearrange the words into sentences.

1️⃣ ①大约　②有　③电梯　④5个　⑤故障 → _____

2 ①乘客 ②有 ③30个 ④轿厢里 ⑤大约 → _____

3 ①大约 ②100毫米 ③长度 ④有 ⑤弹簧 → _____

4 ①高度 ②5米 ③机房 ④有 ⑤大约 → _____

语法点 2 Grammar Point 2

假设复句"如果……，则……" Hypothetical Compound Sentence "如果……，则……"

"如果……，则……" indicates a hypothetical condition. You can also say "如果……，就……". For example,

例句	英文翻译
Rúguǒ yǒu wèntí, zé jìnxíng chǔlǐ. 如果有问题，则进行处理。	If there is a problem, crack it.
Rúguǒ yóubēi sōngdòng, zé yào jìnxíng gùdìng. 如果油杯松动，则要进行固定。	If the oil cup is loose, secure it.
Rúguǒ yóubēi zhōng méiyǒu rùnhuáyóu, zé yào zhùrù rùnhuáyóu. 如果油杯中没有润滑油，则要注入润滑油。	If the oil cup is empty, fill it with lubricant.

用所给的词语造句。Make sentences with the given words.

1 如果油杯有问题，要进行处理。

如果_____，则_____。

2 油杯没有润滑油，就要注入润滑油。

如果_____，则_____。

3 曳引机有振动，就是有故障。

如果_____，则_____。

4 急停开关有故障，不能进入轿顶。

如果_____，则_____。

汉字书写 Writing Chinese Characters

文化拓展 Culture Insight

故宫 The Imperial Palace

The Imperial Palace, serving as the royal palace for both the Ming and Qing dynasties of China, stands as the world's most intact assembly of traditional wooden architectural complexes. Located in the heart of Beijing, the Imperial Palace covers an area of more than 720,000 square meters. It is composed of dozens of courtyards with halls and more than 9,900 rooms. The Imperial Palace follows the time-honored pattern of imperial palaces in ancient China, with its configuration pivoted on the Three Great Halls, demarcating the space into the

第 24 课 | 检查油杯

Outer and Inner Quarters. More than just a symbol of Chinese history and cultural ethos, it stands as a testament to the pride of the Chinese people. It was inaugurated as an all-encompassing museum, housing a wealth of priceless artifacts that reflect the splendor of ancient Chinese civilization.

 小结 Summary

词语 Words

朗读下列词语。Read aloud the following words.

油杯	顶部	处理	方法
问题	大约	摇动	步骤

语法 Grammar

朗读下列句子。Read aloud the following sentences.

1. 油位大约在油杯高度 2/3 的位置。
2. 电梯里面大约有 30 个乘客。
3. 如果有问题，则进行处理。
4. 如果油杯松动，则要进行固定。

课文理解 Text Comprehension

复述课文内容。Retell the text.

1. 检查……。
2. 在轿厢……，检查……；
3. 查看……；
4. 向油杯……，油位……；
5. 用相同的方法……。如果……，则……。

第 25 课 Lesson 25

检查导靴 Jiǎnchá dǎoxuē
Inspect the Guide Shoes

复习 Revision

根据图片选择词语。Choose the words based on the pictures.

1 毛毡（　　）
   钢丝绳（　　）

2 油杯（　　）
   液位（　　）

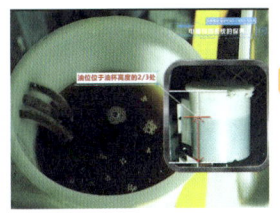

3 油位（　　）
   润滑油（　　）

4 顶部（　　）
   吸附（　　）

225

 热身 Warm-up

看图连线。Look at the pictures and match them with the words.

 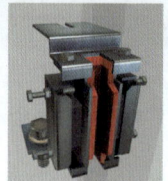 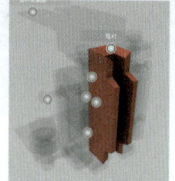 

dǎoxuē	dìngwèixiāo	zàoshēng	xuēchèn
导靴	定位销	噪声	靴衬
guide shoes	locating pin	noise	shoe liner

 学习生词 Words and Expressions 🎧 25-01

1	导靴	dǎoxuē	n.	guide shoes
2	轿厢运行分析仪	jiàoxiāng yùnxíng fēnxīyí	phr.	elevator ride quality analyzer
3	噪声	zàoshēng	n.	noise
4	摆动	bǎidòng	v.	swing
5	对	duì	prep.	to
6	靴衬	xuēchèn	n.	shoe liner
7	只要……,就……	zhǐyào……, jiù……		as long as

8	所有	suǒyǒu	*adj.*	all
9	定位销	dìngwèixiāo	*n.*	locating pin
10	齐全	qíquán	*adj.*	complete, ready
11	紧固	jǐngù	*v.*	tighten

词语练习 Word Exercises

1. 认读词语。Recognize and read the words.

轿厢运行分析仪

导靴

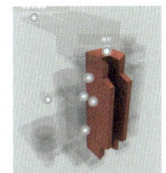

靴衬

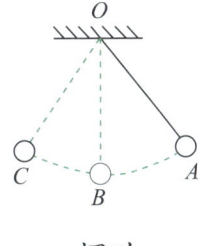

摆动

噪声

定位销

2. 朗读词语搭配。Read aloud the word collocations.

❶ 摆动	轿厢摆动
	对重摆动
❷ 齐全	定位销齐全
	工具齐全

❸ 紧固	紧固螺栓
❹ 内	轿厢内
	机房内

学习课文 Text 🎧 25-02

检查 导靴
Jiǎnchá dǎoxuē

用轿厢运行分析仪在轿厢内测量噪声和摆动。如果有噪声或摆动，要对导靴进行检查。用塞尺测量导轨和靴衬的间隙，只要间隙大于1毫米，就应该更换所有的靴衬。检查定位销是否齐全，导靴是否松动，并紧固螺栓。

Inspect the Guide Shoes

Measure the noise and swing in the car with an elevator ride quality analyzer. If there is a noise or swing, check the guide shoes. Measure the clearance between the guide rail and each shoe liner with a feeler gauge. Replace all the shoe liners as long as the clearance exceeds 1 mm. Check if all the locating pins are ready and the guide shoes are loose. Remember to tighten the bolts.

课文练习 Text Exercises

1. 判断对错。Tell whether the following statements are true (T) or false (F).

   ① 轿厢运行分析仪可以测量噪声。　　　　　　　　　　（　　）
   ② 有噪声和摆动，要检查导靴。　　　　　　　　　　　　（　　）
   ③ 导轨和靴衬的间隙可以大于 1 毫米。　　　　　　　　（　　）
   ④ 导靴松动时，轿厢运行有摆动。　　　　　　　　　　　（　　）

2. 选词填空。Choose the words to fill in the blanks.

   ① 轿厢内不能有（　　）和摆动。　　　A. 声音　　B. 噪声
   ② 用轿厢运行分析仪（　　）噪声。　　A. 检查　　B. 测
   ③ 导靴和靴衬的间隙不能大于（　　）毫米。　A. 1　　B. 2
   ④ 检查定位销是否（　　）。　　　　　A. 齐全　　B. 松动

学习语法 Grammar

语法点 1 Grammar Point 1

动词"进行" The Verb "进行"

It means being engaged in (formal) activities. A sentence usually goes like "进行 + Verb Phrase". For example,

例句	英文翻译
Rúguǒ yǒu zàoshēng huò bǎidòng, yào duì dǎoxuē jìnxíng jiǎnchá. 如果有噪声或摆动，要对导靴进行检查。	Check the guide shoes if there is a noise or swing.
Rúguǒ jiànxì dàyú 1 háomǐ, yào duì xuēchèn jìnxíng gēnghuàn. 如果间隙大于1毫米，要对靴衬进行更换。	Replace the shoe liners as long as the clearance exceeds 1 mm.
Wǒmen yào duì diàntī jìnxíng wéibǎo. 我们要对电梯进行维保。	We need to maintain the elevator.

连词成句。Rearrange the words into sentences.

1 ①万用表 ②对 ③控制柜 ④进行 ⑤检查 ⑥用

→ _____

2 ①电梯工 ②进行 ③电梯 ④对 ⑤维保

→ _____

3 ①进行 ②扳手 ③对 ④靴衬 ⑤更换 ⑥用

→ _____

4 ①检查 ②对 ③进行 ④应急照明 ⑤断开电源

→ _____

语法点 2 Grammar Point 2

条件复句"只要……，就……" Conditional Compound Sentence "只要……，就……"

"只要……，就……" indicates getting a result under a necessary condition. For example,

第 25 课 | 检查导靴

例句	英文翻译
Zhǐyào yǒu zàoshēng huò bǎidòng, jiù yào jiǎnchá dǎoxuē. 只要 有 噪声 或 摆动，就要 检查 导靴。	Check the guide shoes as long as the elevator makes noise and swings.
Zhǐyào jiànxì dàyú 1 háomǐ, jiù yào gēnghuàn dǎoxuē. 只要 间隙 大于 1 毫米，就要 更换 导靴。	Replace the guide shoes as long as the clearance exceeds 1 mm.
Zhǐyào yóubēi zhōng méiyǒu rùnhuáyóu, jiù yào zhùrù. 只要 油杯 中 没有 润滑油，就要 注入。	Refill the oil cup as long as it is empty.

句子连线。**Match the sentences.**

1. 只要导靴松动，   就要检查导靴。
2. 只要检查层门，   就要戴安全帽。
3. 只要轿厢有摆动，   就要紧固螺栓。
4. 只要维保电梯，   就要准备顶门器。

 汉字书写 **Writing Chinese Characters**

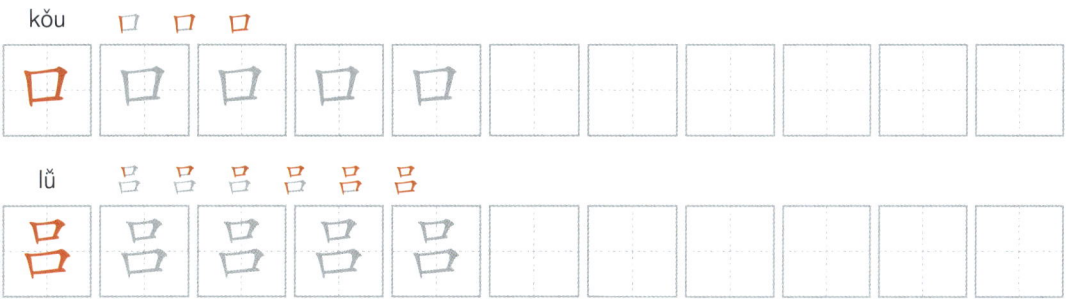

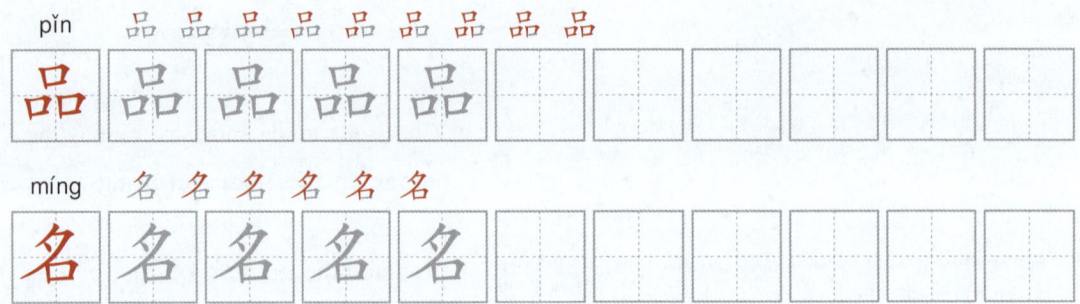

 **职业拓展 Career Insight**

观光电梯 Observation Elevator

Observation elevator, with a car featuring transparent walls, is designed for riders to enjoy panoramic views outside. It can be installed either inside or outside buildings. Observation elevators typically do not require high operational speeds since passengers usually prefer to spend extra time inside the car to appreciate the external views. The car of such an elevator consists of two components: the passenger compartment and the viewing area. The latter is often situated at the rear part of the car, featuring a transparent scenic wall. The surfaces of the exposed parts of an observation elevator need to be smooth, durable and corrosion-resistant.

第 25 课 | 检查导靴

小结 Summary

词语 Words

朗读下列词语。Read aloud the following words.

螺栓	噪声	导靴	摆动
齐全	定位销	紧固	靴衬

语法 Grammar

朗读下列句子。Read aloud the following sentences.

1. 如果有噪声或摆动，要对导靴进行检查。
2. 如果间隙大于 1 毫米，要对靴衬进行更换。
3. 只要有噪声和摆动，就要检查导靴。
4. 只要油杯中没有润滑油就要注入。

课文理解 Text Comprehension

复述课文内容。Retell the text.

1. 用轿厢运行分析仪……。
2. 如果有……，要……。
3. 用塞尺测量……，只要……，就应该……。
4. 检查……，导靴……，并……。

第 26 课 Lesson 26

Tuìchū jiǎodǐng
退出轿顶
Exit the Elevator Car Roof

 **复习 Revision**

根据图片选择词语。Choose the words based on the pictures.

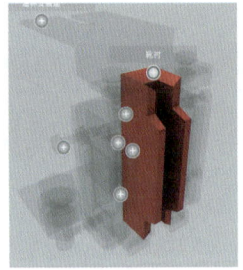

1. 螺栓（　　）
   靴衬（　　）

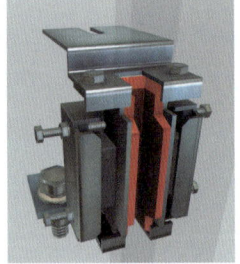

2. 导靴（　　）
   导轨（　　）

3. 齐全（　　）
   噪声（　　）

4. 定位销（　　）
   紧固（　　）

第 26 课 | 退出轿顶

 热身 Warm-up

看图连线。Look at the pictures and match them with the words.

  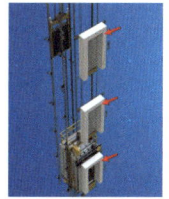 

ānquánmào hòumiàn	pāidǎ céngmén	tíxǐng	diàntī lóucéng
安全帽 后面	拍打 层门	提醒	电梯 楼层
behind the safety helmet	tap at the floor door	remind	elevator floor

 学习生词 Words and Expressions  26-01

1	退出	tuìchū	v.	exit
2	轻	qīng	adj.	lightly, gently
3	拍打	pāidǎ	v.	tap
4	提醒	tí//xǐng	v.	remind
5	离开	lí//kāi	v.	leave
6	根据	gēnjù	prep.	based on, according to
7	不同	bù tóng	phr.	different
8	楼层	lóucéng	n.	floor
9	直接	zhíjiē	adj.	direct

235

| 10 | 该 | gāi | *pron.* | this |
| 11 | 后面 | hòumiàn | *adj.* | following |

词语练习 Word Exercises

1. 认读词语。Recognize and read the words.

安全帽后面　　　　提醒　　　　电梯楼层　　　　拍打层门

2. 朗读词语搭配。Read aloud the word collocations.

❶ 楼层	不同楼层
	相同楼层
❷ 拍打	拍打层门
❸ 退出	退出轿顶

第 26 课 | 退出轿顶

 学习课文 Text 🎧 26-02

退出轿顶
Tuìchū jiàodǐng

退出轿顶前，用手轻轻拍打层门，提醒外面的人离开。拍下急停开关，根据不同情况进行操作：进出轿顶楼层相同时，直接退出轿顶，复位检修开关和急停开关；进出轿顶楼层不同时，先验证该楼层的门锁，再进行后面的操作。

Exit the Elevator Car Roof

Before exiting the elevator car roof, gently tap at the landing door to remind people outside to leave. Tap the stop button and proceed accordingly based on different situations. If the technician steps out of the car roof on the same floor as the one he entered, he can exit the elevator car roof and reset the inspection switch and the stop button. In case the floors differ, he should verify the door lock of the landing floor first, and then continue with the next steps.

237

课文练习 Text Exercises

1. 判断对错。Tell whether the following statements are true (T) or false (F).

   ① 退出轿顶前要拍打层门。 (   )
   ② 退出轿顶时，可以直接出来。 (   )
   ③ 进出楼层不同时，可以直接退出轿顶。 (   )
   ④ 退出轿顶后，复位急停开关。 (   )

2. 选词填空。Choose the words to fill in the blanks.

   ① (   ) 轿顶前，拍打层门提醒外面的人离开。
   　A. 退出　　　　　　　B. 进入　　　　　　　C. 使用
   ② 进出 (   ) 楼层时，直接退出轿顶。
   　A. 不同　　　　　　　B. 相同
   ③ 退出轿顶 (   )，复位急停开关和检修开关。
   　A. 后　　　　　　　　B. 前
   ④ 进出楼层不同时，要先 (   ) 门锁。
   　A. 验证　　　　　　　B. 检查

学习语法 Grammar

语法点 1 Grammar Point 1

介词"根据" The Proposition "根据"

"根据" indicates the reason for actions. A sentence usually goes like "根据 + Noun + Verb Phrase". For example,

例句	英文翻译
Gēnjù bù tóng qíngkuàng jìnxíng cāozuò. 根据不同 情况 进行 操作。	Proceed accordingly based on different situations.
Gēnjù zàoshēng quèdìng yèyǐnjī shìfǒu zhèngcháng. 根据 噪声 确定 曳引机 是否 正常。	Check if the traction machine is normal according to the noise.
Gēnjù jiàoxiāng zàoshēng, jiǎnchá bù tóng de bùjiàn. 根据 轿厢 噪声，检查 不同 的 部件。	Check the different parts according to the noise in the elevator car.

用所给的词语造句。Make sentences with the given words.

1. 查看电压，确定接触器是否要更换。

    根据_____。

2. 老师要求我戴安全帽。

    根据_____。

3. 情况不同，进行的操作不同。

    根据_____。

4. 部件不同，检查的要求不同。

    根据_____。

语法点 2 Grammar Point 2

代词"该" The Pronoun "该"

It refers to the person or thing mentioned before. The word is equivalent to "this", and mainly used in written language. For example,

例句	英文翻译
Gāi céng mén ménsuǒ xūyào yànzhèng. 该 层门 门锁 需要 验证。	The door lock of this floor needs to be verified.

例句	英文翻译
Gāi diàntī de céngmén yǒu wèntí. 该电梯的层门有问题。	There is something wrong with the landing door of this elevator.
Gāi yèyǐnjī yǒu gùzhàng. 该曳引机有故障。	There is something wrong with this traction machine.

选词填空。Choose the words to fill in the blanks.

1. 曳引机有振动，那么（　　）曳引机有故障。　A. 该　　B. 彼此
2. 导轨和靴衬的间隙大于1毫米，则（　　）靴衬要更换。
   　　　　　　　　　　　　　　　　　A. 该　　B. 彼此
3. 电梯维保时，应该确认（　　）电梯的位置。　A. 该　　B. 彼此
4. 进入轿顶前，应该验证（　　）层门的门锁。　A. 该　　B. 彼此

 汉字书写 Writing Chinese Characters

dǎ 打 打 打 打 打
打

pāi 拍 拍 拍 拍 拍 拍 拍
拍

tí 提 提 提 提 提 提 提 提 提 提 提
提

jù 据 据 据 据 据 据 据 据 据 据
据

第 26 课 | 退出轿顶

文化拓展 Culture Insight

中国高铁 High-Speed Railway in China

The high-speed railway system of China, the longest, fastest, and most sophisticated one in the world, is an accomplishment that the nation holds in high esteem. It plays a pivotal role in driving China's economy forward and enhancing its social mobility and efficiency. In 2011, the total length of China's high-speed railway overtook that of all other countries in the world. In 2021, the figure exceeded 40,000 km, connecting almost all the parts of China. Exports of the self-developed Fuxing Trains to multiple countries attest to China's growing clout in the realm of high-speed railway. This is a matter of great pride for Chinese people and is hailed as a miracle of the world. It encapsulates China's strides and capacity for technological innovation, and concurrently manifests China's willingness to engage with the world and espouse a spirit of cooperation.

小结 Summary

 词语 Words

朗读下列词语。Read aloud the following words.

| 退出 | 提醒 | 拍 | 根据 |

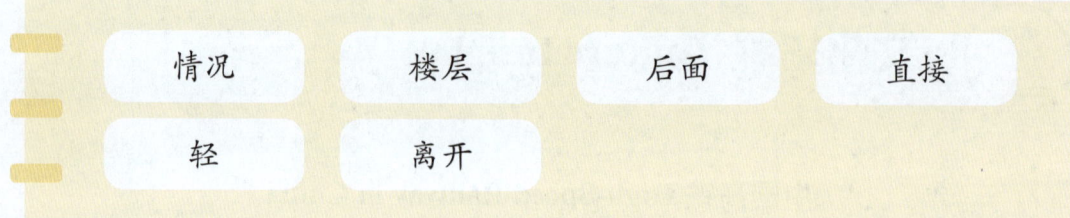

语法 Grammar

朗读下列句子。Read aloud the following sentences.

1. 根据不同情况进行操作。
2. 根据噪声确定曳引机是否正常。
3. 该层门门锁需要验证。
4. 该电梯的层门有问题。

课文理解 Text Comprehension

复述课文内容。Retell the text.

1. 退出……，用手……，提醒……离开。
2. 拍下……，……操作。
3. 进出……时，直接……，复位……和……。
4. 进出……时，先……，再……。

第 27 课 Lesson 27

Cèliáng píngcéng jīngdù
测量平层精度
Test the Landing Accuracy

复习 Revision

朗读下列词语。Read aloud the following words.

退出	提醒	拍	根据
楼层	后面	离开	轻

热身 Warm-up

看图连线。Look at the pictures and match them with the words.

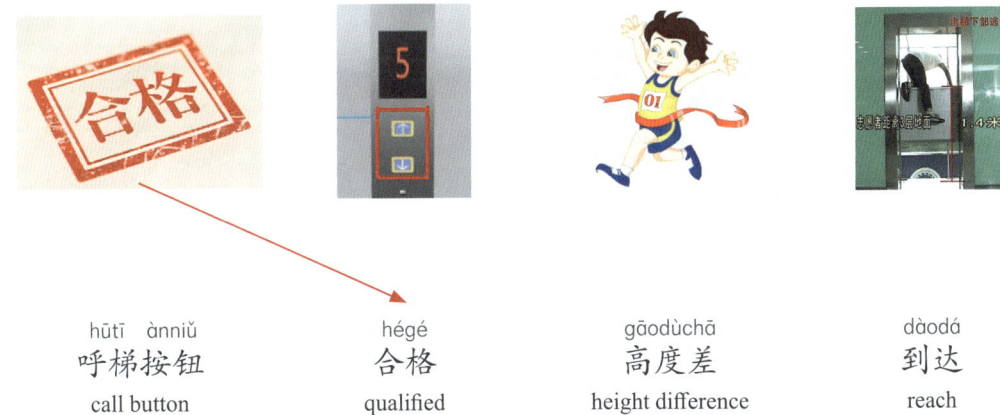

hūtī ànniǔ	hégé	gāodùchā	dàodá
呼梯按钮	合格	高度差	到达
call button	qualified	height difference	reach

学习生词 Words and Expressions 🎧 27-01

1	呼梯按钮	hūtī ànniǔ	*phr.*	call button
2	当	dāng	*prep.*	when
3	到达	dàodá	*v.*	reach
4	地面	dìmiàn	*n.*	ground
5	高度差	gāodùchā	*n.*	height difference
6	精度	jīngdù	*n.*	accuracy
7	合格	hégé	*adj.*	qualified, up to standard
8	调整	tiáozhěng	*v.*	adjust
9	重复	chóngfù	*v.*	repeat
10	这个	zhège	*pron.*	this
11	过程	guòchéng	*n.*	process, procedure

词语练习 Word Exercises

1. 认读词语。Recognize and read the words.

合格

高度差

到达

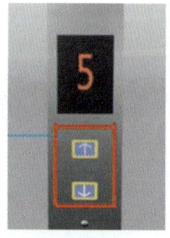
呼梯按钮

2. 朗读词语搭配。Read aloud the word collocations.

❶ 呼梯按钮	按下呼梯按钮	
❷ 平层精度	测量平层精度	
❸ 调整	调整导靴	
❹ 地面	层站地面	
	轿厢地面	

学习课文 Text 🎧 27-02

测量 平层 精度
Cèliáng píngcéng jīngdù

在 顶层，按下 呼梯按钮，当 电梯 到达
Zài dǐngcéng, ànxia hūtī ànniǔ, dāng diàntī dàodá

后，用 直尺 测量 轿厢 地面 和 层站 地面 的
hòu, yòng zhíchǐ cèliáng jiàoxiāng dìmiàn hé céngzhàn dìmiàn de

高度差。高度差小于15毫米，平层精度合格；高度差大于15毫米，平层精度不合格，此时需要调整。重复这个过程，检查所有层站的平层精度。

Test the Landing Accuracy

Press the call button on the top floor. When the elevator reaches, measure the height difference between the car level and the floor level with a ruler. A reading less than 15 mm is considered up to standard. The landing accuracy needs to be adjusted if the reading is greater than 15 mm. Repeat this process to check the landing accuracy of all the floors.

课文练习 Text Exercises

1. 判断对错。Tell whether the following statements are true (T) or false (F).

    ① 从1层开始测量平层精度。（   ）
    ② 高度差是16毫米，平层精度合格。（   ）
    ③ 只需要检查一个楼层的平层精度。（   ）
    ④ 高度差大于15毫米，此时需要调整。（   ）

2. 选词填空。Choose the words to fill in the blanks.

    ① 高度差（   ）15毫米，平层精度合格。   A. 大于   B. 小于

2 (　　) 可以把轿厢呼叫到 1 楼。　　A. 呼梯按钮　　B. 限速器

3 平层精度 (　　)，要进行调整。　　A. 合格　　B. 不合格

4 要测量 (　　) 楼层的高度差。　　A. 一楼　　B. 所有

学习语法 Grammar

语法点 1　Grammar Point 1

介词"当"　The Preposition "当"

Referring to "at a certain time/place", it is often followed by a subject-predicate phrase or a phrasal verb to explain what is happening. It is frequently used in conjunction with words that indicate time, such as "时","时候","前", and "后". For example,

例句	英文翻译
Dāng diàntī dàodá hòu, yòng zhíchǐ cèliáng gāodùchā. 当电梯到达后，用直尺测量高度差。	After the elevator arrives, measure the height difference with a ruler.
Dāng píngcéng jīngdù hégé hòu, zài cèliáng qítā lóucéng. 当平层精度合格后，再测量其他楼层。	After the landing accuracy is up to standard, proceed with other floors.
Dāng píngcéng jīngdù bù hégé shí, yào tiáozhěng gāodùchā. 当平层精度不合格时，要调整高度差。	There is a need to adjust the height difference if the landing accuracy is not up to standard.

2. 选词填空。Choose the words to fill in the blanks.

1 (　　) 电梯困人时，需要盘车救援。　　A. 当　　B. 对于

2 (　　) 导轨的检查，先目测是否变形。　　A. 当　　B. 对于

3 (　　) 高度差小于 15 毫米时，平层精度合格。　　A. 当　　B. 对于

4 (　　) 维保电梯时，需要穿工作服。　　A. 当　　B. 对于

语法点 2　Grammar Point 2

能愿动词"需要"　The Optative Verb "需要"

"需要" is used before a verb and means "to need". (Its negative form is "不用"). For example,

例句	英文翻译
Píngcéng jīngdù bù hégé, xūyào tiáozhěng. 平层 精度 不 合格，需要 调整。	The accuracy of the landing floor needs to be adjusted if it's not up to standard.
Cèliáng gāodùchā xūyào yòng zhíchǐ. 测量 高度差 需要 用 直尺。	We need a ruler to measure the height difference.
Dǎkāi céngmén xūyào sānjiǎo yàoshi. 打开 层门 需要 三角 钥匙。	A triangle key is needed to open the hall door.

连词成句。Rearrange the words into sentences.

1　①电梯　②困人　③当　④需要　⑤盘车救援　⑥时　⑦进行
→ _____

2　①进入　②验证　③门锁　④需要　⑤轿顶
→ _____

3　①平层精度　②层站　③所有　④都　⑤的　⑥检查　⑦需要
→ _____

4　①放　②维保　③需要　④护栏　⑤电梯　⑥时
→ _____

第 27 课 | 测量平层精度

 汉字书写 Writing Chinese Characters

 职业拓展 Career Insight

鼓轮式电梯 Winding Drum Elevator

Winding drum elevators operate on the principle of using a DC motor to power the winch setup involving a worm reducer. This setup winds or unwinds a hoist cable attached at one end to the elevator car. As the drum rotates, it either

draws in or releases the cable, causing the elevator car to rise or descend accordingly. The elevator is simple in structure, whereas the drawbacks include restricted lifting height or loading capacity as well as the poor safety. In 1903, traction elevators started to replace drum-style elevators and took center stage as the most common elevator format.

小结 Summary

词语 Words

朗读下列词语。Read aloud the following words.

精度	高度差	需要	到达
调整	当	过程	合格

语法 Grammar

朗读下列句子。Read aloud the following sentences.

1. 当电梯到达后，用直尺测量高度差。
2. 当平层精度合格后，再测量其他楼层。
3. 平层精度不合格，需要调整。
4. 打开层门需要三角钥匙。

课文理解 Text Comprehension

复述课文内容。Retell the text.

1. 在……，按下……，当……，用直尺……高度差。
2. 高度差小于……，……合格。
3. 高度差大于……，……，此时需要调整。
4. 重复……，检查……平层精度。

第 28 课 Lesson 28

Jiǎnchá guāngmù gōngnéng
检查光幕功能
Inspect the Function of the Light Curtain

 复习 Revision

根据图片选择词语。Choose the words based on the pictures.

❶ 到达（   ）
　 过程（   ）

❷ 合格（   ）
　 调整（   ）

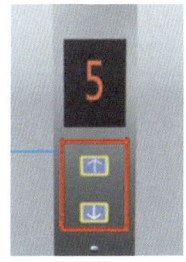

❸ 按钮（   ）
　 呼梯按钮（   ）

❹ 高度差（   ）
　 离开（   ）

251

 **热身 Warm-up**

看图连线。Look at the pictures and match them with the words.

guāngmù	zhēdǎng	jǐngbào	tòumíng
光幕	遮挡	警报	透明
light curtain	block	alarm	transparent

 **学习生词 Words and Expressions** 28-01

1	光幕	guāngmù	n.	light curtain
2	任意	rènyì	adj.	any
3	一	yī	num.	one, first
4	层	céng	m.	floor
5	透明	tòumíng	adj.	transparent
6	物体	wùtǐ	n.	object
7	遮挡	zhēdǎng	v.	block
8	重新	chóngxīn	adv.	again
9	发出	fāchū	v.	give off, make (a sound)

第 28 课 | 检查光幕功能

10	警报	jǐngbào	n.	alarm
11	的话	dehuà	part.	used to follow a hypothetical clause
12	就	jiù	adv.	used to indicate something comes naturally under certain conditions
13	表示	biǎoshì	v.	indicate
14	否则	fǒuzé	conj.	otherwise
15	维修	wéixiū	v.	repair

词语练习 Word Exercises

1. 认读词语。Recognize and read the words.

光幕　　　　　透明　　　　　遮挡　　　　　警报

2. 朗读词语搭配。Read aloud the word collocations.

❶ 遮挡	遮挡光幕	
❷ 维修	维修电梯	
❸ 警报	发出警报	
	警报声音	

253

学习课文 Text 🎧 28-02

检查光幕功能

用呼梯按钮把轿厢运行到任意一层。观察轿厢门是否完全打开。当电梯门关闭时,用不透明物体遮挡轿厢光幕,观察轿厢门是否重新打开,并发出警报。轿厢门能打开和关闭的话,就表示光幕功能正常;否则就表示光幕有故障,需要维修或更换。

Inspect the Function of the Light Curtain

Press the call button to let the elevator car travel to any floor, and check if the elevator car door is fully open. Block the light curtain with an opaque object when the elevator doors are closing, and see if the elevator car door opens again with an alarm. If the car door can still work (open and close) under this circumstance, it indicates that the light curtain is working. Otherwise, it implies a malfunction and needs to be repaired or replaced.

第 28 课 ｜ 检查光幕功能

课文练习 Text Exercises

1. 判断对错。Tell whether the following statements are true (T) or false (F).

   ① 检查光幕功能，在任意一层都能进行。　　　　　　（　　）
   ② 用不透明物体检查光幕功能。　　　　　　　　　　（　　）
   ③ 遮挡轿厢光幕会发出警报。　　　　　　　　　　　（　　）
   ④ 遮挡光幕时，门正常关闭，光幕正常。　　　　　　（　　）

2. 选词填空。Choose the words to fill in the blanks.

   ① 用不透明物体（　　）轿厢门光幕。　　A. 遮挡　　B. 检查
   ② 轿厢门不能正常打开和关闭表示（　　）功能异常。
   　　　　　　　　　　　　　　　　　　　A. 轿门　　B. 光幕
   ③ 用（　　）可以将轿厢运行到任意一层。A. 报警按钮　B. 呼梯按钮
   ④ 光幕不正常的话，需要（　　）或更换。A. 维修　　B. 调整

学习语法 Grammar

语法点 1 Grammar Point 1

……的话，就……

It is used to indicate a hypothetical condition. For example,

例句	英文翻译
Jiàoxiāngmén néng dǎkāi hé guānbì dehuà, jiù biǎoshì guāngmù zhèngcháng. 轿厢门 能 打开和关闭 的话，就表示 光幕 正常。	If the elevator car door can still work (be opened and closed), it indicates that the light curtain is working.

255

(续表)

例句	英文翻译
Yèyǐnjī yǒu zhèndòng dehuà, jiù biǎoshì yǒu gùzhàng. 曳引机有 振动 的话，就表示有 故障。	It the traction machine vibrates, it means there is a breakdown.
Jiàoxiāng yǒu bǎidòng dehuà, jiù yào jiǎnchá dǎoxuē. 轿厢 有 摆动 的话，就要 检查 导靴。	If the car swings, the guide shoe must be inspected.

用所给的词语造句。Make sentences with the given words.

1. 轿厢运行有摆动，要检查导靴。
   _____的话，就_____。

2. 如果进入轿顶，要先验证门锁。
   _____的话，就_____。

3. 退出轿顶前，要先拍下急停开关。
   _____的话，就_____。

4. 检查制动器时，要先断开电源。
   _____的话，就_____。

语法点 2 Grammar Point 2

连词"否则" The Conjunction "否则"

It indicates "if not" and is mostly used in written language. For example,

例句	英文翻译
Wéixiū diàntī shí, bìxū fànghǎo hùlán, fǒuzé bù ānquán. 维修电梯时，必须 放好 护栏，否则 不安全。	When maintaining the elevator, the guardrail must be put in place, otherwise it is not safe.
Wéibǎo shí, yào dài ānquánmào, fǒuzé bù ānquán. 维保 时，要戴 安全帽，否则不安全。	Please wear a safety helmet when maintaining the elevator, otherwise it's not safe.

（续表）

例句	英文翻译
Zhìdòngqì de jiànxì yào bú dàyú 0.7 háomǐ, fǒuzé yào jìnxíng tiáozhěng. 制动器的间隙要不大于0.7毫米，否则要进行调整。	The brake clearance is not greater than 0.7 mm, otherwise it needs to be adjusted.

选词填空。Choose the words to fill in the blanks.

1. 要先释放机械能，（　　）不能检查制动器。　　A. 否则　　B. 则
2. 要先穿绝缘鞋，（　　）不能维保电梯。　　　　A. 否则　　B. 则
3. 表笔接触后，万用表有声音，（　　）表示正常。A. 否则　　B. 则
4. 导轨没有变形，（　　）要进行更换。　　　　　A. 否则　　B. 则

汉字书写 Writing Chinese Characters

gāng
冈 冈 冈 冈 冈

tóng
同 同 同 同 同 同

nèi
内 内 内 内

ròu
肉 肉 肉 肉 肉 肉

 文化拓展 Culture Insight

筷子 Chopsticks

Chopsticks are truly a pair of magical things. They are thin, long and upright, like twin dancers gracefully performing on a dining table. Chopsticks are not simply tableware; they reflect the essence of Chinese culture. Light and flexible, they allow people to pick up and enjoy the delectable Chinese food. Using chopsticks requires certain skills and patience, but once mastered, they can bring joy and  a sense of accomplishment. Chopsticks remain an indispensable element either in the warmth of a family feast or the formality of a business dining event. They bear witness to the Chinese culinary culture and also convey the wisdom and emotional ties of Chinese people.

 小结 Summary

 词语 Words

朗读下列词语。Read aloud the following words.

| 遮挡 | 重新 | 透明 | 任意 |
| 光幕 | 否则 | 物体 | 维修 |

第 28 课 | 检查光幕功能

语法 Grammar

朗读下列句子。Read aloud the following sentences.

1. 轿厢门能打开和关闭的话,就表示光幕正常。
2. 轿厢有摆动的话,就要检查导靴。
3. 轿厢门能打开和关闭的话,表示光幕功能正常,否则需要维修或更换。
4. 维修电梯时,必须放好护栏,否则不安全。

课文理解 Text Comprehension

复述课文内容。Retell the text.

1. 用……把轿厢……。观察轿厢门……。
2. 当……时,用不透明物体……,观察轿厢门……,并……。
3. 轿厢门能……,就表示……;否则……,需要……。

第 29 课 Lesson 29

Cèliáng jiàomén jiànxì
测量轿门间隙
Measure the Elevator Car Door's Clearances

复习 Revision

朗读下列词语。Read aloud the following words.

遮挡	重新	透明	任意
光幕	否则	物体	维修

热身 Warm-up

看图连线。Look at the pictures and match them with the words.

shàngbian　　cāozòng miànbǎn　　sījī zhuàngtài　　liǎng cè　　xiàbian
上边　　　　操纵 面板　　　　司机 状态　　　　两 侧　　　下边
upper side　　operating panel　　"Attendant Control" mode　　two sides　　lower side

 学习生词 Words and Expressions 29-01

1	首先	shǒuxiān	adv.	first
2	操纵面板	cāozòng miànbǎn	phr.	operating panel
3	使	shǐ	v.	let, make
4	处于	chǔyú	v.	be, stay
5	司机状态	sījī zhuàngtài	phr.	"Attendant Control" mode
6	以下	yǐxià	n.	(the) following
7	侧	cè	n.	side
8	上边	shàng biān	phr.	upper side
9	下边	xià biān	phr.	lower side
10	超过	chāoguò	v.	exceed
11	标准	biāozhǔn	n.	standard

词语练习 Word Exercises

1. 认读词语。Recognize and read the words.

上边

下边

操纵面板

两侧

2. 朗读词语搭配。Read aloud the word collocations.

❶ 测量	测量门和门之间的间隙	
	测量上边和轿厢之间的间隙	
	测量下边和地面之间的间隙	
	测量门和两侧之间的间隙	

学习课文 Text 🎧 29-02

Cèliáng jiàomén jiànxì
测量 轿门 间隙

Shǒuxiān guānbì jiàomén, ránhòu dǎkāi diàntī cāozòng miàn-
首先 关闭 轿门，然后 打开 电梯 操纵 面
bǎn, ànxia kāiguān, shǐ diàntī chǔyú sījī zhuàngtài. Yòng
板，按下 开关，使 电梯 处于 司机 状态。用

第 29 课 | 测量轿门间隙

<ruby>塞<rt>sāi</rt></ruby><ruby>尺<rt>chǐ</rt></ruby><ruby>测<rt>cè</rt></ruby><ruby>量<rt>liáng</rt></ruby> <ruby>以<rt>yǐ</rt></ruby><ruby>下<rt>xià</rt></ruby> 4 <ruby>个<rt>gè</rt></ruby> <ruby>间<rt>jiàn</rt></ruby><ruby>隙<rt>xì</rt></ruby>：<ruby>门<rt>mén</rt></ruby> <ruby>和<rt>hé</rt></ruby> <ruby>门<rt>mén</rt></ruby> <ruby>之<rt>zhī</rt></ruby><ruby>间<rt>jiān</rt></ruby>、<ruby>门<rt>mén</rt></ruby> <ruby>和<rt>hé</rt></ruby> <ruby>两<rt>liǎng</rt></ruby><ruby>侧<rt>cè</rt></ruby> <ruby>之<rt>zhī</rt></ruby><ruby>间<rt>jiān</rt></ruby>、<ruby>门<rt>mén</rt></ruby> <ruby>的<rt>de</rt></ruby> <ruby>上<rt>shàng</rt></ruby> <ruby>边<rt>biān</rt></ruby> <ruby>和<rt>hé</rt></ruby> <ruby>轿<rt>jiào</rt></ruby><ruby>厢<rt>xiāng</rt></ruby> <ruby>之<rt>zhī</rt></ruby><ruby>间<rt>jiān</rt></ruby>、<ruby>门<rt>mén</rt></ruby> <ruby>的<rt>de</rt></ruby> <ruby>下<rt>xià</rt></ruby> <ruby>边<rt>biān</rt></ruby> <ruby>和<rt>hé</rt></ruby> <ruby>轿<rt>jiào</rt></ruby><ruby>厢<rt>xiāng</rt></ruby> <ruby>地<rt>dì</rt></ruby><ruby>面<rt>miàn</rt></ruby> <ruby>之<rt>zhī</rt></ruby><ruby>间<rt>jiān</rt></ruby> <ruby>的<rt>de</rt></ruby> <ruby>间<rt>jiàn</rt></ruby><ruby>隙<rt>xì</rt></ruby>。<ruby>间<rt>Jiàn</rt></ruby><ruby>隙<rt>xì</rt></ruby> <ruby>都<rt>dōu</rt></ruby> <ruby>不<rt>bù</rt></ruby> <ruby>超<rt>chāo</rt></ruby><ruby>过<rt>guò</rt></ruby> 6 <ruby>毫<rt>háo</rt></ruby><ruby>米<rt>mǐ</rt></ruby>，<ruby>则<rt>zé</rt></ruby> <ruby>符<rt>fú</rt></ruby><ruby>合<rt>hé</rt></ruby> <ruby>标<rt>biāo</rt></ruby><ruby>准<rt>zhǔn</rt></ruby>。

Measure the Elevator Car Door's Clearances

First, close the car door. Uncover the elevator's operating panel, press the button to switch it into the "Attendant Control" mode. Measure the four clearances as below with a feeler gauge — the one between doors, the one between the door and the two sides (the door jambs), the one between the upper side of the door and the elevator car, and the one between the door's lower side and the floor of the elevator car. They meet the standards if the clearances do not exceed 6 mm.

课文练习 Text Exercises

1. 判断对错。Tell whether the following statements are true (T) or false (F).

   1. 测量轿厢间隙要关闭轿门。　　　　　　　　　　　　（　　）
   2. 要用塞尺测量轿门间隙。　　　　　　　　　　　　　（　　）
   3. 标准要求间隙不超过 6 毫米。　　　　　　　　　　　（　　）
   4. 对于轿门，需要测量 4 个位置的间隙。　　　　　　　（　　）

2. 选词填空。Choose the words to fill in the blanks.

1. 门与门之间的间隙不超过（　　）毫米。
   A. 6　　　　　　　　B. 5

2. 打开操纵面板后，让电梯处于（　　）。
   A. 司机状态　　　　　B. 检修状态

3. 门与门之间的间隙是7毫米时，（　　）标准。
   A. 符合　　　　　　　B. 不符合

4. 门的上边、（　　）和两侧的间隙都要测量。
   A. 下行　　　　　　　B. 下边

学习语法 Grammar

语法点1 Grammar Point 1

……，使……

It means "to cause a certain result". A sentence usually goes like "使 + Noun + Verb/Adjective Phrase". For example,

例句	英文翻译
Ànxià kāiguān, shǐ diàntī chǔyú sījī zhuàngtài. 按下开关，使电梯处于司机状态。	Press the button to switch the elevator into the "Attendant Control" mode.
Duànkāi diànyuán, shǐ diàntī tíngzhǐ yùnxíng. 断开电源，使电梯停止运行。	Disconnect the power supply to stop the elevator.
Yājǐn huǎnchōngqì, shǐ duìzhòng tíngzhǐ xiàxíng. 压紧缓冲器，使对重停止下行。	Press the buffer to prevent the counterweight from going down.

连词成句。Rearrange the words into sentences.

1. ①按下　②运行　③使　④电梯　⑤按钮

　→ _____

2 ①松开 ②使 ③对重 ④制动器 ⑤下行

→ _____

3 ①急停开关 ②使 ③电梯 ④正常 ⑤复位 ⑥运行

→ _____

4 ①调整 ②使 ③它（it） ④符合 ⑤标准 ⑥间隙

→ _____

语法点 2 Grammar Point 2

方位词"之间" The Directional Word "之间"

"之间" indicates a point/state somewhere between two locations, time, persons, things, or quantities. For example,

例句	英文翻译
Yòng sāichǐ cèliáng mén yǔ mén zhījiān de jiànxì. 用塞尺测量门与门之间的间隙。	Measure the clearance between the doors with a feeler gauge.
Duìyú jiàomén, yào cèliáng mén hé liǎng cè zhījiān de jiànxì. 对于轿门，要测量门和两侧之间的间隙。	Measure the clearance between the elevator car door and the two sides (the door jambs).
Yào cèliáng mén de xiàbiān hé diàntī dìmiàn zhījiān de jiànxì. 要测量门的下边和电梯地面之间的间隙。	Measure the clearance between the lower side of the door and the elevator's floor.

选词填空。**Choose the words to fill in the blanks.**

1 首先测量门与门（　　）的间隙。

　　A. 上边　　　　B. 以下　　　　C. 之间

2 用塞尺测量（　　）4个间隙。

　　A. 上边　　　　B. 以下　　　　C. 之间

3. 用塞尺测量柱塞顶杆和制动臂（　　）的间隙。
   A. 上边　　　　　　　B. 以下　　　　　　　C. 之间

4. 用直尺测量对重和缓冲器（　　）的距离。
   A. 上边　　　　　　　B. 以下　　　　　　　C. 之间

 汉字书写 Writing Chinese Characters

 职业拓展 Career Insight

双轿厢电梯 Double-Deck Elevator

The world's first double-deck elevator was installed by Otis in 1931 at the Empire State Building in New York. This elevator design includes a pair

of vertically connected cars, which can transport passengers on two floors at the same time. It amplifies the load capacity, optimizes the shaft usage, and ramps up the overall mobility within the building. A notable milestone was reached when, in 1968, Otis installed a groundbreaking double-deck elevator system in Chicago. The system integrated a dozen double-deck elevators and four standalone single-deck ones. This innovation solidified Otis's position at the forefront of elevator advancements, offering an inventive response to the logistical needs of tall structures.

小结 Summary

词语 Words

朗读下列词语。Read aloud the following words.

上边	下边	司机状态	处于
地面	超过	首先	使
侧	标准		

语法 Grammar

朗读下列句子。**Read aloud the following sentences.**

1. 按下开关,使电梯处于司机状态。
2. 压紧缓冲器,使对重停止下行。
3. 用塞尺测量门和门之间的间隙。
4. 用塞尺测量门和两侧之间的间隙。

课文理解 Text Comprehension

复述课文内容。**Retell the text.**

1. 首先关闭……,然后打开……,按下……,使……。
2. 用塞尺……:……之间、……之间、……之间、……之间的间隙。
3. 间隙都不超过……,……。

第 30 课 Lesson 30

Gēnghuàn ànniǔ
更换按钮
Replace the Button

复习 Revision

根据图片选择短语。Choose the phrases based on the pictures.

（　）　　　　　　　　　（　）

（　）　　　　　　　　　（　）

A. 测量门和门之间的间隙　　　B. 测量门的上边和轿厢之间的间隙
C. 测量门的下边和地面之间的间隙　　D. 测量门和两侧之间的间隙

 ## 热身 Warm-up

看图连线。Look at the pictures and match them with the words.

liánshang	chāichú	diànxiàn	bádiào
连上	拆除	电线	拔掉
connect	remove, uninstall	wire	unplug

 ## 学习生词 Words and Expressions 🎧 30-01

1	一旦	yídàn	conj.	once
2	发现	fāxiàn	v.	find, discover
3	无效	wúxiào	v.	malfunction, break down, be ineffective
4	立即	lìjí	adv.	immediately
5	拔掉	bádiào	phr.	unplug
6	电线	diànxiàn	n.	wire
7	拆掉	chāidiào	phr.	remove, uninstall
8	安装	ānzhuāng	v.	install
9	连	lián	v.	connect

10	它	tā	pron.	it
11	有效性	yǒuxiàoxìng	n.	effectiveness, validity

词语练习 Word Exercises

1. 认读词语。Recognize and read the words.

电线　　　　　　拆掉　　　　　　连上　　　　　　拔掉

2. 朗读词语搭配。Read aloud the word collocations.

❶ 掉	拔掉电线	
	拆掉按钮	
	拆掉光幕	
❷ 按钮	按钮无效	
	按钮有效	
❸ 安装	安装电梯	

学习课文 Text 🎧 30-02

更换 按钮
Gēnghuàn ànniǔ

一旦发现轿厢的按钮无效,就需要立即更换。首先断开电梯电源,然后打开电梯操纵面板,拔掉无效按钮的电线并拆掉按钮,接着安装上新按钮并重新连上电线,再恢复电梯电源,按下按钮,验证它的有效性。

Replace the Button

Once the button of the elevator car is found malfunctioning, it is necessary to replace it immediately. First, disconnect the power supply, then uncover the operating panel, and unplug the button from its wires. Replace the non-functioning button with a new one, reconnect it with the wires, and then restore the elevator power. Press the button to verify whether it is properly working.

课文练习 Text Exercises

1. 判断对错。Tell whether the following statements are true (T) or false (F).

  ① 电梯按钮无效，不需要立即更换。　　　　　　　　　　（　　）
  ② 更换按钮时，不需要断开电源。　　　　　　　　　　　（　　）
  ③ 更换按钮时，要先拆掉再安装。　　　　　　　　　　　（　　）
  ④ 安装新按钮后，需要验证按钮是否有效。　　　　　　　（　　）

2. 选词填空。Choose the words to fill in the blanks.

  ① 断开电梯电源后，打开电梯（　　　）。　　A. 轿厢　B. 操纵面板
  ② 拔掉电线，（　　　）无效的按钮。　　　　A. 拆掉　B. 连上
  ③ 重新连上电线，再（　　　）电梯电源。　　A. 关闭　B. 恢复
  ④ 更换好新按钮后，要（　　　）新按钮的有效性。 A. 恢复　B. 验证

学习语法 Grammar

语法点1 Grammar Point 1

一旦……，就……

It indicates a hypothetical condition and is often used to present unfavorable scenarios that might occur. For example,

例句	英文翻译
Yídàn ànniǔ wúxiào, jiù yào gēnghuàn ànniǔ. 一旦按钮无效，就要更换按钮。	Once the button is malfunctioning, it is necessary to replace it immediately.
Yídàn yǒu zàoshēng huò bǎidòng, jiù yào jiǎnchá dǎoxuē. 一旦有噪声或摆动，就要检查导靴。	Once noise and swings are detected, it is necessary to check the guide shoes.

（续表）

例句	英文翻译
Yídàn yóubēi méiyǒu rùnhuáyóu, jiù yào zhùrù rùnhuáyóu. 一旦油杯没有润滑油，就要注入润滑油。	Once the oil cup is empty, it is necessary to refill it.

用所给的词语造句。**Make sentences with the given words.**

1. 发现按钮无效，就要更换按钮。

    一旦_____，就_____。

2. 如果电梯困人，就要盘车救援。

    一旦_____，就_____。

3. 如果导靴松动，就要紧固螺栓。

    一旦_____，就_____。

4. 如果平层精度不合格，就要调整。

    一旦_____，就_____。

语法点 2 Grammar Point 2

动词 + 掉   V + "掉"

"掉" is a resultative complement. The structure indicates the completion of an action. Here it means "to remove". For example,

例句	英文翻译
Bádiào wúxiào ànniǔ de diànxiàn. 拔掉无效按钮的电线。	Unplug the malfunctioning button from its wires.
Bǎ ànniǔ chāidiào, zài ānzhuāng shang xīn de ànniǔ. 把按钮拆掉，再安装上新的按钮。	Remove the button and replace the old button with a new one.
Diàntīgōng rēngdiào wúxiào de ànniǔ. 电梯工扔掉无效的按钮。	The elevator worker threw away the malfunctioning button.

选词填空。Choose the words to fill in the blanks.

1. 更换按钮，首先要断（　　）电源。
   A. 掉　　　　B. 开　　　　C. 下　　　　D. 上

2. 打开操纵面板，拔（　　）无效按钮的电线。
   A. 掉　　　　B. 开　　　　C. 下　　　　D. 上

3. 连（　　）按钮电线后，再恢复电源。
   A. 掉　　　　B. 开　　　　C. 下　　　　D. 上

4. 按（　　）按钮，验证它的有效性。
   A. 掉　　　　B. 开　　　　C. 下　　　　D. 上

 汉字书写 Writing Chinese Characters

huā

cǎo

chá

yá

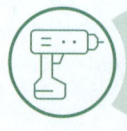

文化拓展 Culture Insight

网络购物 Online Shopping

Online shopping is simply a digital carnival in China! Countless things, ranging from home appliances, smart devices to food and fashion wear, are just a click away. Empty the shopping cart, and just pick them up at the door step — what a magic! Moreover, economical prices with guaranteed quality make people feel confident in their buys and enjoy a hassle-free user experience. Besides the advantages of speed and simplicity, e-shopping often comes with unexpected treats such as flash sales and coupon discounts. In today's digital landscape, online shopping has expanded people's choices and enriched their experiences.

小结 Summary

 词语 Words

朗读下列词语。Read aloud the following words.

发现	拔掉	拆掉	连
恢复	无效	电线	它

语法 Grammar

朗读下列句子。Read aloud the following sentences.

1. 一旦按钮无效，就要更换按钮。
2. 一旦有噪声和摆动，就要检查导靴。
3. 拔掉无效按钮的电线。
4. 把按钮拆掉，再安装上新的按钮。

课文理解 Text Comprehension

复述课文内容。Retell the text.

1. 一旦发现……，就需要……。
2. 首先断开……，然后打开……，拔掉无效按钮的……并……。
3. 接着安装上……并……。
4. 再……，……，验证……。